"If you have a vague sense t
riencing, if you find yours
methodology of prayer, or if you simply want to take a step closer to God in prayer, John Koessler has provided us with a window into his own journey and struggles with prayer. Whether you agree with all of his conclusions or not, Mr. Koessler provides a map to explore this most important issue for any person trying to converse with God."

KURT BJORKLAND, senior pastor, Orchard Hill Church

"John Koessler is right when he labels prayer an awkward conversation. For many of us, this insight alone will help us gain clarity about the act of praying. The discussion on the dimensions of prayer that take place in each chapter provides definition to this conversation, instruction, and encouragement about our awkward, extraordinary communion with God which is the practice of prayer."

SCOTT GIBSON, professor of preaching and holder of the David E. Garland Chair of Preaching, George W. Truett Theological Seminary

"Talking with God, assured he's listening, is at the heart of our relationship with the One who knows us best and loves us perfectly. But is there a child of God who hasn't struggled with prayer? I relaxed in the good company of John Koessler as he put to words my thoughts and questions to make me comfortable with the silence of God as the presence of God. Whether praying feels too familiar or even strange, John's honest insights invite us to pray—not by prescribing mere methods but by reminding us of the God who hears."

DEBBIE DICKERSON, managing editor of *Mature Living*

"Even though I've been a believer for many years, I've always had the feeling that everyone else was better at praying than me. John Koessler's book assures me that I am not alone. Sometimes prayer is hard, and it can often feel like, as John labels it, an 'awkward conversation.' Yet, as Christ followers, prayer is our lifeline, our sustaining nourishment, our solace in grief, our escape from worry. Prayer elevates us out of the ordinary, refocusing our hearts on God. *When God Is Silent* is filled with down-to-earth advice and captivating storytelling that will revitalize your prayer life."

JAMIE JANOSZ, managing editor of *Today in the Word*

"I have read countless books on prayer, a tribute to both my deep need and dogged belief. I return to only two or three. This is a book to read and return to. Building on scripture and the best books on prayer, John Koessler, writing in quotable prose, adds his sometimes brutally honest, sometimes deeply poignant experiences and insights. He gets between the lines of our questions, leaving us with a sense of God's goodness and welcome every time we come to Him."

ROSALIE DE ROSSET, professor of literature and homiletics,
Moody Bible Institute

When God Is Silent

Let the Bible Teach You to Pray

When God Is Silent

Let the Bible Teach You to Pray

JOHN KOESSLER

LEXHAM PRESS

When God Is Silent: Let the Bible Teach You to Pray

Copyright 2023 John Koessler

Lexham Press, 1313 Commercial St., Bellingham, WA 98225
LexhamPress.com

Print ISBN 9781683597025
Digital ISBN 9781683597032
Library of Congress Control Number 2022949541

Lexham Editorial: Deborah Keiser, Allisyn Ma, Jordan Short, Mandi Newell
Cover Design: Brittany Schrock
Typesetting: Abigail Stocker

For Jane, who prays better than anyone I know.

Contents

Introduction

C. S. Lewis once observed that he had never come across a book on prayer that was of any use to him. He said that he had seen many books of prayers, but when it came to books about prayer, the writers usually made the wrong assumptions about the reader. Or, at least, they made the wrong assumption about him. "The author assumes that you will want to be chatting in the kitchen when you ought to be in your cell," he observes. "Our temptation is to be in our studies when we ought to be chatting in the kitchen." [1]

I have often felt something similar. Books about prayer don't seem to fit my situation. They either assume that I don't *want* to pray or that I don't know *how*. Neither is really the case. My problem lies elsewhere. I don't like the experience of talking to God when I pray. Our conversations seem awkward.

I have been praying as long as I have been a Christian. Longer, even. I've never felt that my problem with prayer was a matter of mechanics. Prayer never seemed like rocket science to me—you just talk to God. When I became a pastor, I became a praying professional. That is to say, prayer was a part of my job. I prayed publicly as the church worshiped. I opened board meetings with prayer. I led the church's weekly prayer meeting. I prayed for the congregation in my study. And I prayed with those who came to me for counsel. Over time I discovered that most people are like me. We pray, sometimes frequently, but there is something about the experience that leaves us feeling awkward. We aren't sure why.

After giving this question thought over many years, it seems to me that many of the problems we have with prayer have nothing to do with motivation or method. They are the sort of problems that we might describe as relational.

How do you carry on a conversation with someone who never seems to talk back to you? Why do I feel like God is unresponsive to my requests?

I don't always get what I want when I pray, and even when I do, it rarely takes the form that I anticipate. What do I do about the anger I sometimes feel toward others or even toward God himself? Is that a safe subject to talk about? Does God feel cheated when I pray the prayers of other people? Am I being lazy if I do? Does he view those prayers as a form of spiritual plagiarism?

I am a person of faith, but I've never thought of myself as a person of great faith. If I had been with Peter when he asked to walk on water, I'd have stayed in the boat. If Peter had asked me about his request in advance, I probably would have discouraged him. I doubt that anyone would call me a spiritual adventurer. Given this fact, what does faith look like for an ordinary person like me? How much faith is enough to validate my prayers?

Finally, how should we pray in this chatterbox age in which we live? It's not surprising that everyone has an opinion, but I sometimes grow weary of their assumption that I want to hear it. I know that God probably doesn't share my sentiment, but what happens when distress, discouragement, or grief delivers us to a place where our words fail us? How shall we pray then?

In the end, the secret to prayer is not a matter of method or even motive. The key to prayer is God himself. I have written this book to do more than answer questions like those I have mentioned above. It is my hope—indeed, it is my *prayer*—that as you read, you will also gain a sense of God, of his goodness, and the rich welcome that is waiting for you every time you approach him in the name of Jesus Christ.

Chapter 1

Awkward Conversations with God

Silence is the language of the seemingly absent God.
—*Lynn R. Szabo*

Our family's first pet was an abandoned German shepherd pup. We found him in a box in our local Casey's parking lot, a pump-and-go general store on the edge of town. He was so tiny and cute that we couldn't bear to leave him. We named him Casey for obvious reasons, but he was a bad dog. He chewed the carpet and growled at babies. When Casey bit someone, we realized we couldn't keep him. It was difficult but not nearly as hard as the task of telling my two little boys. I choked out the sad news between gasps and tears, trying to explain why it was necessary.

Some conversations are just hard: telling someone about the loss of a loved one; talking to the kids about the facts of life; informing an employee that their contract will not be renewed; making small talk with a person with whom you have virtually nothing in common. It's not always easy. But for me, nothing is quite as challenging as trying to talk with someone who has nothing to say. You know the kind of conversation I mean. This is the sort where you do all the heavy lifting while the other person responds with an impenetrable silence. In a way, a one-sided conversation is an oxymoron. We might call it a monologue, a soliloquy, or a sermon, but whatever it is, it is not a conversation.

Not everyone is a good conversationalist. Some of us are shy. We have thoughts, many good ones, but we may have trouble expressing those thoughts to others. Some of us are distracted, too busy thinking about other things that we do not listen to what the other person is saying, while others like to talk so much that they do not make room for the silence necessary for another person to join in. At times, we think we are having a conversation when we are merely holding forth. We are mostly interested in what we have to say. To count as a conversation, an exchange of thought between at least two people is required.

God Is Not Much of a Conversationalist

I say this to make a point about God, or to be more precise, to make a point about my experience with

God in prayer. I have not found God to be much of a conversationalist.

He is mostly silent when I talk to him. Not that I am a great conversationalist either. My prayers are repetitive, usually made up of the same requests every time. My attention span is short. I tend to fall asleep too. I suppose that if I were on the other side of the conversation, I would probably be too bored to respond myself. But at least I say something. God, as far as I can tell, doesn't have anything to say. I make an effort to pray, and it seems that all I get in return is an awkward silence. "OK then," I say. "I guess I'll be on my way."

We know from Scripture that God has a voice. According to the book of Genesis, the first words ever spoken were God's words: "God said, 'Let there be light,' and there was light" (Genesis 1:3). Yet, the Bible also shows that God is no chatterbox. God indeed spoke to Moses "face to face, as one speaks to a friend" (Exodus 33:11). He spoke to Abraham the same way, but ordinary conversation has never been God's primary communication mode, at least not the kind of conversations we are used to having. He has chosen to speak through others most of the time: prophets, preachers, and occasionally angels. Even then, God has never shown himself to be what you could describe as voluble. His words have been, for the most part, relatively few and sometimes far between. Long gaps of years, decades, centuries, and even millennia separate the occasions where God speaks to his people.

Taken as a whole, God's words provide enough material to fill the Old and New Testaments. But when considered individually, those instances where God has spoken exhibit two main characteristics that make conversation, as we usually understand it, complicated. One is a feature we might describe as deference. Most of the time, God does not speak to us directly. Instead of speaking in his own voice, God has spoken through human agents who were "carried along by the Holy Spirit" (2 Peter 1:21). By communicating in this manner, God was doing what Israel had asked him to do on Mount Sinai. When Israel heard God's voice, they were so put off by the experience that they begged him to stop. God came to Elijah in a gentle whisper, but on Sinai, it was with a shout and in a blaze of fire. "Go near and listen to all that the LORD our God says. Then tell us whatever the LORD our God tells you," they begged Moses. "We will listen and obey" (Deuteronomy 5:27). We assume that it would be a comfort to hear God speak directly to us. Yet Scripture suggests that we are more likely to be unnerved by the experience. Perhaps, like Job, we would want to put our hands over our ears in stunned silence (Job 40:3–5).

The other characteristic of God's verbal communication is restraint. Although God has spoken at many times and in various ways, he is not garrulous. His words tend to be few and far between. When God does speak, he does not say everything that could be said. We are sometimes frustrated by this reserve. There is much we would like to know. Of course, we know there are probably good reasons for the things God chooses not to tell us. Would we understand them even if he told us? Sometimes we have a question, and Scripture bluntly tells us that the answer is none of our business (Acts 1:7; Romans 9:19–20). We think we would feel better if God told us everything we wanted to know, but is this true?

Would knowing why God answered our prayer in a disappointing way make that answer easier to accept?

We think the answer is yes, even though the same experience on a purely human level has repeatedly proven otherwise.

Sometimes when God has spoken to his servants, he seems to leave out details that we would consider important. The nativity of our Lord is a good example of what I mean. God sends an angel to announce to Mary that she will conceive a child by the Holy Spirit, who will be the Son of God (Luke 1:26–38). He also sends an angelic messenger in a dream to reassure her future husband, Joseph, that the whole plan is from God and that he shouldn't be afraid to take Mary as his wife (Matthew 1:18–23). Yet God does not tell them that the child is supposed to be born in Bethlehem instead of Nazareth, where they currently live. This detail not only required a journey of some ninety miles but was also necessary for the fulfillment of Scripture. This failure to mention the child's designated birthplace seems like a significant omission to most of us. Yet God appears to have been content to leave it to circumstances to make sure that the couple was in the right place at the right time. Specifically, it took a decree from the Roman emperor that a census be taken "of the entire Roman world" to get them into place in time (Luke 2:6).

Curiously, the Gospel writers do not seem to be bothered by this. If anything, Luke sees the decree as part of a larger body of evidence proving that God was at work. As if Luke wants us to know where God's plan is concerned, the LORD does not need help. He will move heaven and earth to bring about what he has promised.

The New Testament record of Jesus's words may be the most comprehensive example we have of God speaking in a conversational way. This record includes dialogues, monologues, sermons, and even a few prayers. But even this is incomplete. At the end of his Gospel, John admits that if all the things Jesus did were written down, "the whole world would not have room for the books that would be written" (John 21:25). The information included in the Gospels is not an exhaustive biography, but it is narrowly focused on the three-year span in Jesus's life that culminated in his crucifixion and resurrection.

This same economy is on display in the beginning of the book of Acts, where Luke mentions that Jesus appeared to the disciples over a span of forty days "and spoke about the kingdom of God" (Acts 1:3). Yet Luke reveals nothing about what Jesus actually said about the subject. Presumably, Jesus left it to the apostles to pass that information on to us.

All this is typical of what theologians call "special revelation." First, as the label suggests, special revelation was *special*. It was not an everyday occurrence. Taken as a whole, the Bible describes many occasions where God revealed himself to specific individuals, but very few had a face-to-face conversation with him (Exodus 33:11; Numbers 12:8). As the writer of Hebrews observes, "In the past God spoke to our ancestors through the prophets at many times and in various ways, but in these last days he has spoken to us by his Son, whom he appointed heir of all things, and through whom also he made the universe" (Hebrews 1:1–2).

Second, instances of special revelation were relatively narrow in their focus, reserved primarily for those events and individuals that advanced God's redemptive plan. They were not meant to serve as models of the way God usually speaks to us. Most believers do not hear a voice, see a vision, or encounter an angel. God speaks to us through the Scriptures, the written record of divine self-revelation.

In addition to this, there is the awkwardness created by the imbalance of power between ourselves and God. You might think that this would be an encouragement. In one of his hymns, John Newton urges those who pray to bring requests large enough to be worthy of God's might: "You are coming to a king—large petitions with you bring. For His grace and pow'r are such, none can ever ask too much, none can ever ask too much."[1] But we often have the opposite reaction when contemplating God's sovereignty. Theologian Helmut Thielicke describes the chilling effect it can have: "Have not all of us, down in the secret corners of our hearts become a bit fatalistic and so tend to forego the feeble gesture of prayer, which, after all, is only the whimpering of a child in a storm and does not avert the storm anyhow?"[2]

Or instead of becoming fatalistic and giving up, we grow agitated. Instead of dwelling on God's power, we shift the focus to ourselves. We fret about the frequency of our prayers and their tone, convinced that it would guarantee the result if we could find the right level of intensity. This may look like devotion, but it is the opposite. "Don't you see that all your efforts, your chattering of empty phrases, your crying is like battering down a door that is already open?" Thielicke asks. "Don't you see what a terrible distrust this is of him who opened the door and is waiting for you, as did the father of the prodigal son?"[3]

Prayer as Extraordinary Conversation

Whatever prayer may be, it is not an ordinary conversation. Someone has called prayer "primary speech," but it is not like any speech we hear from other people.[4] If prayer is a conversation, it is a unique kind of conversation. Believers in every generation have understood prayer as one of the means by which God communicates to his people. Yet it is a conversation where we do the majority of the talking. In prayer, we approach God but do not see either face or form and do not hear his voice. Therefore it is a conversation that lacks all the normal cues we rely upon for meaning. When we talk to God, we cannot rely upon inflection, body language, or facial expression to gauge his response the way we can when conversing with others.

Prayer differs from ordinary conversation in another respect. Those who pray often talk to themselves as well to God. Sometimes this takes the form of self-talk or self-encouragement. As Martyn Lloyd-Jones observes, it is an effort to "take ourselves in hand" and proclaim the truth to yourself. "Have you realized that most of your unhappiness in life is due to the fact that you are listening to yourself instead of talking to yourself?" Lloyd-Jones asks.[5]

The self-talk of prayer is not a pep talk or even positive thinking. When we talk to ourselves in prayer, we remind ourselves of the truth we already know. We remember God's disposition toward us and base our expectations upon it. This kind of prayer talk amounts to a confession of faith made in the presence of God. We ground our assertions in revelation and experience as we review what God has already told us in his word. We consider how he has dealt with us in the past. Based on these things, we put our expectations into words and speak them aloud. "Why, my soul, are you downcast? Why so disturbed within me? Put your hope in God, for I will yet praise him, my Savior and my God" the psalmist prays in Psalm 42:5 (see also Psalm 42:11; 43:5).

At other times we put into words the answers we expect to receive from God (Psalm 35:3; 71:21). We repeat to ourselves what we know to be true about God and our situation. We pray back to ourselves the promises of God as if God were speaking them directly to us.

Sometimes the answers we form for ourselves in prayer are based on feelings and impressions. These may reflect God's assurance, but they are not infallible.

If we are honest with ourselves, we will admit that when we come to prayer, it is not with a request so much as with a plan. Our prayers not only include an ask but directions on how the answers should come. In this way, what some have called "listening prayer" all too often becomes a presumptuous prayer. We bring our desires and plans with us to prayer and then place them on God's lips.

In 2 Samuel 7, David decided to build a temple for God. David had constructed a palace for himself and was enjoying a time of peace, but when he noticed the disparity between his dwelling and the tabernacle that housed the ark of the covenant, it bothered him. The king called for the prophet Nathan. "Here I am, living in a house of cedar, while the ark of God remains in a tent," he said (2 Samuel 7:2). David had not even shared the details of what he was planning when the prophet responded: "Whatever you have in mind, go ahead and do it, for the LORD is with you" (2 Samuel 7:3). It made sense. David's ambition was noble. He wanted to honor God, who had already shown that he was with David. It seemed reasonable to both men that David's plan was also pleasing to God. But that night, the Lord spoke directly to

Nathan and told him that David would not be the one
to build the temple. The Lord's message to Nathan is
significant, not only because of its verbal nature but its
length. It is "the longest recorded monologue attributed
to him since the days of Moses."[6] What is even more
striking is that both David and Nathan were wrong in
their assumption about what God would do. Neither
was a spiritual lightweight.

If it was easy for them to project their will onto God,
how much more can it be said of us? How often do the
feelings and impressions that we have in prayer corre-
spond to the stirrings of our own desires? Feelings and
impressions have a place, but they are not the only, and
perhaps not even the primary, means that God uses to
guide or speak with us. We do not need to be afraid of
our feelings, but we do need to question them. We can
easily mistake our enthusiasm for a particular course of
action as God's leading. Prayer is the place to disclose
our hearts to God. We express our deepest desires, but
we should not necessarily trust them. We assume that
what we want is what God wills for us simply because
we want it. Even when our requests align with God's will,
we cannot assume that we know how God should grant
them to us. His timing or means of bringing the answer
to pass may be very different than our expectations.

One-Directional Conversation

If prayer is not a conversation in the ordinary sense, then what is it? Prayer is a conversation that moves primarily in one direction. It moves from the believer who prays to the God who hears. God's silence does not mean that he is unresponsive. Listeners are silent when they are paying attention. It is true that in ordinary conversation, silence can also mean other things. When we try to talk to others, they may respond with the silence of disinterest, rejection, or even complete absence. But when it comes to prayer, the first assumption of faith is that we have God's attention: "This is the confidence we have in approaching God: that if we ask anything according to his will, he hears us. And if we know that he hears us—whatever we ask—we know that we have what we asked of him" (1 John 5:14–15).

The one guarantee we have in prayer is that God always hears us. There is more to this hearing than awareness of our requests. The key to understanding John's bold and frequently misunderstood promise is to note that to "hear," in this sense, means something more than to take notice of something. To hear as John uses the term is to grasp the full implications of something. God knows both our desire and our true need. He also knows how our request fits into his plan.

The condition that our requests must be "according to his will" is not an escape clause designed to protect God's reputation if we find the answer to our prayer disappointing. This condition implies our responsibility to consider the nature of the request before we make it. Do we have a warrant to ask such a thing of God? Is it something for which he has told us to pray? How does the request fit with a larger understanding of God's general will and plan for our lives? What is our motive in asking?

God's hearing of our prayers includes an assessment of everything that lies behind them. God's apparent silence when we pray leaves us with the wrong impression. We believe that we are the initiators in prayer and that God stands by impassively as we wait to see what he will do for us. The Scriptures paint a different picture. They show that God moved in our direction first. "The first word is God's word," Eugene Peterson explains. "Prayer is a human word and is never the first word, never the primary word, never the initiating and shaping word simply because we are never first, never primary." For this reason, Peterson describes prayer as "answering speech."[7]

Consequently, prayer is our conversational answer to what God has already said. It responds to his invitation, extended to us through Jesus Christ, to express our needs and desires directly to him. The fact that God does not answer in kind when we speak to him in prayer does not mean that God has nothing to say. As the hymn writer declares, "What more can He say than to you He hath said, You, who unto Jesus for refuge have fled?"[8]

Many Christians look to Scripture to find a method of prayer. There is certainly nothing wrong with this, but we may be so fixated on the technique that we miss the message. Scripture is an essential companion to prayer, not only because it tells us how to pray but because it shows us how the conversation began. The Bible tells us what God has already said. In the process, we do learn something about how to pray. But more importantly, we develop a way of thinking. We begin to understand the one to whom we are speaking.

The trouble with talking is that it is so easy to do. Speech seems only to take a puff of breath and a slip of the tongue. But this is an illusion. That kind of speech is merely blathering. It is the sort of speech that Jesus describes as "babbling" prayer (Matthew 6:7). We have all had experience with this sort of conversation. Someone is talking, but they are not talking to us. Instead, they are talking at us or perhaps about us. We may be present and within hearing range, but we are not really in view. Indeed, the one who is doing the talking is not even listening to themselves. They don't need to. They have recited this litany of complaints or opinions so

often that they don't even have to know what they are
saying to say it.

Prayer as Communion

If the temptation of the theologian is to reduce God
to a topic, the temptation of the spiritual practitioner
is to reduce God to an object. When we objectify God,
we look to him not for a relationship but an experience. Our interest in him extends no further than the
potential he offers to get us what we want. Instead, "The
essence of Christian prayer is to seek God," John Stott
has observed. "We seek him in order to acknowledge
him as the person he is, God the Creator, God the Lord,
God the Judge, God our heavenly Father through Jesus
Christ our Savior."[9]

In other words, although we are tempted to accuse
God of being unresponsive to our prayers because we
cannot hear his voice, the truth is that we are the ones
who are disengaged. He has spoken first, but we do not
take his words into account. We only know what we
want. I am not saying that we have never read the Bible
or even have no interest in God, only that we are sin-
gle-minded in our interests. We have not bothered to
consider God's point of view. We are waiting for him to
respond to us when he has been waiting for us all the
while. We are waiting for him to say something new

without orienting our prayer to what he has already said. What more can he say than he has already said? What would we say differently if we really believed that he was listening? It might help if we thought of prayer as communion instead of conversation.

The essence of communion is shared experience. The mistake we make is to interpret God's silence as absence or disinterest. In true conversation, listening is interaction as much as speech. Listening may even be more of an exchange than words because, to really listen, we must enter into someone's experience. We have all had conversations with those who spoke without really hearing what we were saying. We ourselves have been guilty of this. Such conversations were not a conversation at all but merely an exchange of sounds. In human relationships, silence is a frequent companion of presence.

The Christian idea of communion is rooted in the biblical concept of *koinonia*, a Greek word that means fellowship or sharing. Sometimes *koinonia* speaks of our experience with God and, at other times, of our experience with other believers. There is a connection between these two. In 1 Corinthians 1:9, the apostle Paul reminded the Corinthians that God had called them "into fellowship with his Son, Jesus Christ our Lord." Such language denotes a special kind of relationship. It is a fellowship or union with Jesus Christ. The church celebrates this relationship when it observes the Lord's Supper, a rite that we often call "communion." But the spiritual communion Paul speaks of in 1 Corinthians 1:9 is something more. Fellowship with Christ is an abiding union with our savior. Those who have been called by God and have trusted in Christ are themselves "in Christ Jesus" (Romans 8:1).

This is what Jesus prayed for when he asked that all those who believe "may be one, Father, just as you are in me and I am in you" (John 17: 21). He went on to ask, "May they also be in us so that the world may believe that you have sent me. I have given them the glory that you gave me, that they may be one as we are one." This is often described as a prayer for unity, and unity is partly in view. But Jesus is asking for much more.

In this prayer, Jesus describes two related spheres of relationship. One is a relationship with the Father, Son, and (by implication) the Holy Spirit. Using his relationship with the Father as an analogy, Jesus prayed that those who believe would "also be in us." The other sphere is the relationship believers have with other believers. When Jesus asks that they may be one, he isn't just praying that they will be united, but for their union. There is a difference. Union is a state of being, while unity is a condition. Unity is a responsibility. Union is a gift. There is also an order in these two spheres. Unity between believers is only possible because of the union they share with one another. In turn, that union is a result of the union they have with the Father and the Son and the Spirit.

Our mistake has been to see Jesus's words as a statement of aspiration. Interpreted this way, Jesus's words are more of a wish than a prayer. If desire was all that Jesus meant, he might as well have said, "Father, I hope that they will be one." Indeed, this is how we usually hear this text preached in church. The emphasis is not on what God has done in response to Jesus's prayer, but what we are supposed to do if it is ever going to be a reality. Instead of a prayer addressed to the Father, we have changed it into a sermon preached to the church. The "may be" of verse 21 is not a maybe. It is a "let it be" that echoes the Father's declarations at creation. Just as God said, "Let there be light," and there was light, Jesus prayed, "Let them be one in us and in one another." Because of Jesus, communion with God is a fact, not an aspiration.

What does any of this have to do with our prayers? It means that communion is a state before it is an experience. This communion is a fact even when we are unable to sense its reality. Sometimes when we pray, we feel like we need to do something to attract God's attention. We are like a person on the ground waving their hands at a plane passing high overhead, hoping that someone up there will see us. God does not have to come down from on high to take note of us. We do not need to arrest his attention. Although we often talk about "coming" into God's presence, the truth is that we are already there. Whenever we pray, and even when we are not praying, we are in the Father and the Son and the Spirit.

Our expectations in prayer must be grounded in biblical truth rather than feeling. We do not have to hear God's voice to communicate effectively with God. We are not trying to capture God's attention but responding to an overture that he has already made. Not only was God the first to speak, he spoke to us long before we ever uttered a word to him. He has revealed himself in creation and by his written word. We do not need to feel God's presence to know that he is present when we pray. Psalm 139 assures us that wherever we are, God is already there. "Where can I go from your Spirit? Where can I flee from your presence?" the psalmist says. "If I go up to the heavens, you are there; if I make my bed in the depths, you are there" (Psalm 139:7–8). Indeed, Jesus's prayer reveals that the access we have to God's presence is even deeper than the psalmist imagined. Not only are we always in his presence, but we are also in him, and he is in us.

The awkwardness of prayer should not put us off. It does not originate with God but with us. We have felt uncomfortable with other conversations we have had and have pushed through the discomfort to say what needed to be said. How much more should this be true when it comes to God? "You discern my going out and my lying down; you are familiar with all my ways," the psalmist declares. "Before a word is on my tongue you, LORD, know it completely" (Psalm 139:3–4). We do not need to feel that God is near to be in his presence. We do not need to be comfortable to pray. We do not need to speak nicely to be heard. Before we have even uttered a word, God knows our minds and hearts completely.

Chapter 2

Praying and Getting What
You Want . . . or Not

If you remain in me and my words remain in you,
ask whatever you wish, and it will be done for you.
This is to my Father's glory, that you bear much fruit,
showing yourselves to be my disciples.
—John 15:7–8

I sometimes worry that I am a mercenary when it comes
to prayer. My satisfaction seems contingent on whether I
get what I want. If God grants my request, I am pleased. If
he doesn't, I am frustrated. The desire to get answers to our
prayers seems base. I am embarrassed to be so utilitarian
where God is concerned. Something tells me that my spiritual aspirations should rise higher. No doubt, they should.
But the desire to get something from God is so common
that Jesus addressed it more than once in his teaching.

In one of his parables, Jesus compared prayer to someone who asks a neighbor to loan him three loaves of bread
when an unexpected visitor shows up at midnight (Luke
11:5–8). In the scenario that Jesus describes, the neighbor
is unwilling at first. "Don't bother me," the neighbor says.
"The door is already locked, and my children and I are in
bed. I can't get up and give you anything." What is Jesus's
counsel in such a situation? Keep asking. Be shameless
in your persistence: "I tell you, even though he will not
get up and give you the bread because of friendship, yet
because of your shameless audacity he will surely get up
and give you as much as you need" (Luke 11:8).

Jesus made the same point in another parable "to show
[his disciples] that they should always pray and not give
up" (Luke 18:1). This story concerned a widow who kept
going to a judge with the plea, "Grant me justice against
my adversary" (Luke 18:3). Because the judge "neither
feared God nor cared what people thought," the woman
came to him repeatedly without getting the answer she
desired. The power dynamics described in this witty story
aptly describe how we often feel when it comes to prayer:
helpless, powerless, and frequently ignored.

Is God Reluctant?

Jesus's primary point, of course, is that God is *not*
like the judge. But it is an important starting point to

acknowledge that we often feel that he is. We do not struggle with prayer because it is hard. Our problem is that we are not sure it is worthwhile. We suspect that God is not interested in our case or fear that he will not decide matters in our favor. Delay and denial are the major reasons for this uncertainty. We pray, but the answer does not seem to come. Or we pray, and the response we receive is not the one we had wanted.

Not long after I started following Christ, my mother became so sick that my father had to carry her to the car to drive her to the doctor. Unable to diagnose my mother's condition, the doctor admitted her to the hospital, where she grew worse. All the Christians I knew at the time believed that miraculous healing was a common occurrence. I decided that it must be God's plan to heal her. Like the blind man in John 9:3, I thought God had allowed her sickness "so that the works of God might be displayed" in her. What better way to show my parents the truth of the gospel and bring them both to Christ?

With my heart pounding, I went to the hospital to stand by her bedside and pray, but nothing seemed to happen. Instead of getting better, over the next few days, she grew worse. And then she died. But I continued to pray, thinking that what God had in mind must be even more remarkable than I imagined. I had read about Jesus raising the dead in the Gospels. Maybe that's what he planned to do. My father had asked the funeral director for a closed casket ceremony. But if God could move the stone from Jesus's grave, surely that would be no obstacle. I prayed on. I think you can guess how this story turned out. God did not raise my mother from the dead.

Someone has said that prayer moves the hand that moves the world. But if we think that means we can force God's hand by praying, personal experience will quickly show otherwise. To me, prayer often seems more like a discipline of waiting than an act of call and response. I am not saying that God never grants my requests. He does. But he rarely seems quick about it. God takes his time. Days, weeks, months, and even years may go by without any signs of movement on his part. The irony, or perhaps I should say awkwardness, of this is that Jesus claimed that God is *not* slow. In the parable of the persistent widow, Jesus promised not only that God hears those "who cry out to him day and night," but that he will "see that they get justice, and quickly" (Luke 18:7–8). It seems that my definition of what constitutes delay and God's definition disagree.

What, then, are we to make of the apparent contradiction between God's haste and our experience? Those who say "prayer changes things," tend to lay the blame at our feet. God can do anything, they say. If prayers go unanswered, it is the prayer's fault, not his. The reason must be an insufficient faith on the part of the person or a lack of perseverance. Maybe they have a secret sin or some other spiritual impediment that places an obstacle in the way of God's answer. The power is God's, yet somehow, at least for them, the people praying seem to be the key that unlocks that power.

Jesus's parable implies the opposite. The answer depends upon God. This is precisely why Jesus urges his disciples not to give up. Where the widow is concerned, all the power lies in the hands of others. She cannot protect herself against her adversary, and she cannot control the judge. Despite the helplessness of her position, she displays a kind of brazenness through her persistence. She keeps coming back to the judge with her plea, despite his repeated refusals. Why would anyone do such a thing? It couldn't have been based on her confidence in the judge's character or his sympathy. The only plausible explanation is that it was her helplessness that made her persevere. She had no one else to turn to. Jesus's point in this parable is really a counterpoint.

The key that unlocks the parable is the language of the widow's petition. Most of the translations say that the woman asked for *justice* against her adversary. We immediately think of this as a request with a terminal point. She is looking for revenge. She wants the judge to render a decision against her opponent and finish the matter once and for all. Most of the prayers we pray are like this. They are not prayers for vengeance, but they are terminal in that they have a specific fulfillment in view. We want a particular job. We want God to heal our disease, or maybe we need money to pay a bill. There is nothing wrong with such requests. Quite the opposite, it was Jesus who taught us to pray for daily bread (Matthew 6:11; Luke 11:3). No request could be more concrete than this.

But the widow's request was actually a plea for ongoing protection. "What the widow was seeking was not fundamentally vengeance on her adversary, but relief from his oppressions," theologian B. B. Warfield explains in an essay on this parable. Although there may have been punishment inflicted on the man, Warfield notes, "Punishment was not the main end aimed at or obtained; it was only the means by which the real end of relief and protection was secured."[1] In other words, the widow's request was essentially for what we would today call a "protective order" against her enemy. The essence of the widow's plea is for ongoing protection rather than a terminal solution. "The meaning is 'preserve me against his attacks,' rather than 'deliver me out of his power,'" Warfield points out.[2]

Warfield also notes that "a great strength of emphasis" is placed on the word "quickly" in the parable. When

Jesus asks whether God will bring about justice for his chosen ones or keep putting them off, "the outcome of the whole question and answer is thus the assurance that God will not—not merely leave his elect unavenged, but—be slow to rescue them from their distresses."[3] Whenever we pray, God hears and hastens to answer. We have Jesus's word on this!

Why God Seems Slow

So why does God seem so slow when Scripture assures us that he is *not* slow? One reason is that our relationship to time is very different from God's. He does not experience the limitations of time as we do. As Psalm 90:2 observes, he exists as God "from everlasting to everlasting." The eternal God can act within time as we know it, but he is not bound by time as we are. The Bible uses human experience as a point of reference when talking about his eternal nature. In 2 Peter 3:8, we are told to remember that "with the Lord a day is like a thousand years, and a thousand years are like a day." What seems to us like a delay is not a delay to God. Our physical life has a beginning and an end. God has neither. The apostle goes on to say, "The Lord is not slow in keeping his promise, as some understand slowness. Instead he is patient with you, not wanting anyone to perish, but everyone to come to repentance"

(2 Peter 3:9). God's timing is not our timing because he acts according to his own plan. God fulfills his promises and answers our prayers in a way that suits his greater purpose.

The fact that time does not limit God does not mean that he has no sense of timing. God's plans unfold according to his schedule. Jesus began his public ministry with the words, "The time has come" (Mark 1:15). Romans 5:6 tells us that Christ died for sinners "at just the right time." We are frustrated with the timing of God's answers to our prayers because we forget that we are also part of a larger drama. Prayer often involves waiting. But God, who is eternal and has a unique relationship to time, sees the situation differently. We capture a glimpse of his perspective in the Bible's designation of Jesus Christ as "the Lamb who was slain from the creation of the world" (Revelation 13:8). Scripture uses this language for other aspects of God's redemptive plan as well. The kingdom of God is an inheritance "prepared for you since the creation of the world" (Matthew 25:34). Those who are in Christ were chosen "before the creation of the world to be holy and blameless in his sight" (Ephesians 1:4). Perhaps most significant is the statement of Hebrews 4:3, which says that God's works "have been finished since the creation of the world." From God's perspective, all the details of his purposes and plans have already been fulfilled, even when they have yet to unfold in our time.

In these verses, creation seems to be the demarcation that separates what we call time from eternity past. At his incarnation, Jesus entered into the experience of created time and subjected himself to its limitations. He was miraculously conceived by God in the virgin's womb but developed like any other child until "the time came" for his delivery (Luke 2:6). Once born, the child Jesus "grew in wisdom and stature, and in favor with God and man" (Luke 2:52). Jesus lived out his earthly life in a succession of moments and days. His ministry unfolded in stages (John 2:4; 7:8). During that ministry, Jesus recalled the past and looked ahead to the future. He urged his disciples to "remember" certain events and teachings (Matthew 16:9; John 15:20). He commanded them to observe the Lord's Supper "in remembrance of me" (1 Corinthians 11:24–25). He looked forward to the restoration of his glory (John 17:5). Jesus even prayed to be spared the cup of suffering he was about to undergo, if possible (Matthew 26:39, 42; Mark 14:36; Luke 22:42).

In Christ, God not only tangibly enters the realm of what we would call "real" time but mysteriously draws us with him into eternity by uniting us with the Savior in his redemptive work. Ephesians 2:4–7 says that God "made us alive with Christ even when we were dead in transgressions." As a result, God has "seated us with him in the heavenly realms in Christ Jesus." This involves more than the spiritual bookkeeping that transfers our guilt to him and his righteousness to us. An exchange of our sin for Christ's righteousness is surely included (2 Corinthians 5:21), but there is more implied in these words. The apostle does not speak of these matters as if they are something which we are waiting to take place. He writes about them as things that have already happened and says that they happened to us!

All those who belong to Christ inhabit both time and eternity. On the one hand, they continue to live in the temporal world. In Ephesians 2:7, Paul speaks of "the coming ages" when the incomparable riches of God's grace, expressed in God's kindness toward us, will be put on display. Simultaneously, the apostle depicts those in Christ as already seated with Christ in the heavenly realms in some mysterious way. As far as our daily experience is concerned, we continue to live on a timeline that unfolds as past, present, and future. We are subject to the limitations of the temporal realm in this present life. Yet, we are also living in the reality of Christ's finished work. Our lives have been folded into Christ and his kingdom. As a result, "in all things God works for the good of those who love him, who have been called according to his purpose" (Romans 8:28).

One implication of this is that our prayers' answers are an accomplished fact even before they have been granted. Our participation is both a matter of privilege and a reflection of God's desire that we be in a relationship with him. "It is not really stranger, nor less strange, that my prayers should affect the course of events than that my other actions should do so," C. S. Lewis observes. "They have not advised or changed God's mind—that is, His over-all purpose."[4] Another is that we can be certain that whatever form God's answer may take, it will reflect his loving purpose for our lives. This heavenly perspective casts Jesus's promise in Matthew 18:19 in a new light: "Again, truly I tell you that if two of you on earth agree about anything they ask for, it will be done for them by my Father in heaven." Although the context of Jesus's promise in this particular verse is narrow—it primarily has to do with the exercise of church discipline—it is one of several similar declarations (see Matthew 21:22; Mark 11:24; John 14:13–14). What Jesus describes in these statements is not a positive attitude but a sphere of authority.

Those who ask in faith can be certain of an answer because they operate out of the heavenly realm where

God's will is always done (Matthew 6:10; Luke 11:2; see also Matthew 26:42).

God's Right to Refuse

At this point, we need to acknowledge that the remarkable things Jesus says about prayer have sometimes been misunderstood as a blank check that guarantees that we can get whatever we want from God. The trouble with this understanding is twofold. First, it shifts the focus of prayer away from the Heavenly Father so that our only concern is the particular request we happen to be making. In this type of praying, God is little more than a delivery system for the thing we hope to obtain. He might as well be a vending machine. Second, such an approach confuses an affirmative with an answer. It fails to allow for the possibility that God could also answer our prayer by denying our request. While a "no" is probably not the answer we want, it is still an answer. The folly of those who preach the prosperity gospel is their assumption that we always know best how God should answer our prayers. We are not the best judges of what we need. We certainly do not have enough perspective to know what the timing of God's answers to our prayers should be. We are naturally inclined to be narrow in our desires, selfish in our motives, and short-sighted in our assumptions.

Furthermore, the Bible offers examples of notable saints whose prayers were refused by God. Moses pleaded with God to allow him to enter the land of promise (Deuteronomy 3:23–27). David asked God to heal his first son by Bathsheba (2 Samuel 12:16–20). Paul repeatedly prayed for God to remove the "thorn in my flesh" (2 Corinthians 12:7–9). Most notably, Jesus prayed to be spared the suffering of the cross in language that suggests he was fully aware that such a thing was not possible.

Likewise, there are many in Scripture who waited many years, some for their entire lives, without seeing God grant their desires. Of them, the author of Hebrews writes, "These were all commended for their faith, yet none of them received what had been promised, since God had planned something better for us so that only together with us would they be made perfect" (Hebrews 11:39–40). Although he is not speaking explicitly of prayer, the principle is just as true. The fact that God does not give us our heart's desires as soon as we would like may not mean that he will not give it to us at all. His refusal to grant a request altogether isn't always a sign that God is displeased with us. It doesn't necessarily mean that we lack the faith to receive it. Sometimes God's decision not to grant our request has nothing to do with us at all, at least as far as cause and effect are concerned.

In an essay entitled "The Efficacy of Prayer," C. S. Lewis observes that we should not think of those who get what they pray for as court favorites who have more influence with God than others. "The refused prayer of Christ in Gethsemane is answer enough to that," Lewis points out.[5] The obvious corollary to this is that if we do *not* get what we pray for, we should not automatically assume that we are under God's disfavor or stand on the margins of his interest. Disappointment with God's response to our prayers is at least common enough that Jesus felt it was necessary to urge his disciples not to give up on prayer.

The question remains, however, is it possible for us to sabotage our own prayers? Is there ever a time when we don't get what we ask because it is our own fault? The answer is yes. James 4:2–3 explains, "You desire but do not have, so you kill. You covet but you cannot get what you want, so you quarrel and fight. You do not have because you do not ask God. When you ask, you do not receive, because you ask with wrong motives, that you may spend what you get on your pleasures." James's assertion that his readers do not have because they do not ask sounds like a contradiction to the promises of Jesus that God knows what we need before we ask. Is God so petty that he would overlook a genuine need simply because we have not expressed it? James means something else. If we take the whole statement into account, it quickly becomes clear that what James is describing is not an ask at all. They ask but with impure motives. Indeed, what James describes in these verses is almost a competition. Their prayers are driven by the same desires that cause them to covet, quarrel, and fight with one another.

Prayer is not magic. It does not work like an incantation. We do not get what we want simply because we voice our desire aloud to God. There is a kind of assurance in what James says here. It means that we cannot manipulate God by our prayers. We never have to worry that God will give us something that we should not have. At the same time, the scenario that James describes should sober us because it shows how evil motives can subvert a spiritual activity like prayer. The specific motives mentioned by James are greed and envy. But other motives can insert themselves into our praying. For example, Jesus warns of the danger of praying "to be seen by others" (Matthew 6:5). Some prayers are not prayers at all. They are theater. The prayers Jesus condemns in this verse were public displays of piety intended to elicit praise from others. He warns that such prayers go unanswered: "Truly I tell you, they have received their reward in full."

Other prayers are more like sermons. Although they appear to be addressed to God, they are aimed at those who are within earshot. We sometimes hear these prayers in church services and prayer meetings. The one who prays takes the opportunity to exhort the congregation. These prayers are filled with phrases like, "Lord, I pray that we might …" or "Lord, let us …" Although it may sound like a public confession, this is often a form of indirect criticism. What separates these prayers from real confession? It is that the person praying usually excludes himself from the transgressions being mentioned. Instead of praying, he is voicing his pet peeves aloud in the hearing of the congregation. These prayers are not answered any more than the ones Jesus singles out in Matthew 6:5 for the simple reason that they are not prayers. The speaker is addressing the congregation instead of God. If God is addressed at all, it is only so that the one who prays may tattle on the rest.

What about the problem of prayerlessness? Why do some fail to ask God for what they need? In some cases, it is because they are too independent. They are so used to fending for themselves that it does not occur to them to go to God. Independence may also mask pride. After Adam and Eve disobeyed in the garden of Eden, their first impulse was not to turn to God for help. Instead, they tried to handle the matter themselves. Once they realized that they were naked, "they sewed fig leaves together and made coverings for themselves" (Genesis 3:7).

The Lord showed the inadequacy of these measures by action rather than words. Instead of leaving them in the coverings they had made for themselves, "The LORD God made garments of skin for Adam and his wife and clothed them" (Genesis 3:21). This action may have been partly symbolic. It seems to foreshadow the sacrificial system, which, in turn, pointed forward to Jesus Christ, "the Lamb of God, who takes away the sin of the world" (John 1:29). But God's provision of clothing was also wonderfully practical. The problem was spiritual, but its entrance into human experience also had practical consequences. For one thing, it made clothing necessary. Few needs are as basic as clothing. Jesus included clothing in his list of the core concerns which occupy our minds and cause us to be anxious: "So do not worry, saying, 'What shall we eat?' or 'What shall we drink?' or 'What shall we wear?' For the pagans run after all these things, and your heavenly Father knows that you need them" (Matthew 6:31–32).

The fact that God replaced the flimsy coverings Adam and Eve had made for themselves with garments of skin points to the inadequacy of their initial attempt to take care of this themselves. This provision is all the more striking when we consider that God seems to have done this for them without being asked. Our Heavenly Father knows what we need before we ask him

(Matthew 6:8). Scripture's simple assertion that God made clothes for Adam and Eve gives us the warrant to bring all our mundane concerns to him as well. We do not need to worry that such things are too earthly or too small for his consideration. What was already clear in Eden became even clearer when God became flesh and took his place among us in the person of Jesus Christ. Jesus knew what it was like to be tired, hungry, and thirsty (John 4:4–7). The Son of Man "came eating and drinking" (Matthew 11:19; Luke 7:34). He had "no place to lay his head" (Matthew 8:20; Luke 9:58). No wonder he taught his disciples to pray for "daily bread" (Matthew 6:11). "When we pray to him for daily bread and when we 'little people' are permitted to talk to him about such 'little things,' this does not dishonor his divinity, but it does transfigure the trivialities," theologian Helmut Thielicke observed.[6]

How We Should Pray

The garments of Eden elevate all our trivial concerns. Jesus's teaching on this matter is straightforward. We are not to concern ourselves with things like food and clothes beyond measure. We should not run after them the way the pagans do, but not because such things are of no concern. Rather, we should not be anxious about such things because God knows what we need better than we do. He knows our needs before we are even aware of them.

THE FIRST PRINCIPLE IN PRAYER IS TO ASK

Tell God what you want, as simply as you can:

> Is anyone among you in trouble? Let them pray. Is anyone happy? Let them sing songs of praise. Is anyone among you sick? Let them call the elders of the church to pray over them and anoint them with oil in the name of the Lord. And the prayer offered in faith will make the sick person well; the Lord will raise them up. If they have sinned, they will be forgiven. Therefore confess your sins to each other and pray for each other so that you may be healed. The prayer of a righteous person is powerful and effective. (James 5:13–16)

Getting something from God is not the only thing. But it is the first thing. Need and desire provide the initial impetus for us to pray. There is no reason to be ashamed of this. "We do not need to put on a show of being above the little and the big things in our life," Helmut Thielicke observes. "God wouldn't believe us anyhow."[7]

THE SECOND PRINCIPLE IS TO PRAY HONESTLY

One of the greatest temptations in prayer is to tell God what we think he wants to hear instead of what is really on our heart. The foolishness of such hypocrisy is laid bare by the psalmist who admits to God, "Before a word is on my tongue you, LORD, know it completely" (Psalm

139:4). There is no point in putting on airs. "It is no use
to ask God with factitious earnestness for A when our
whole mind is in reality filled with the desire for B,"
C. S. Lewis advises. "We must lay before Him what is
in us, not what ought to be in us."[8]

THE THIRD PRINCIPLE
OF PRAYER IS TO PERSIST

This advice comes directly from Jesus. Pray and do not
give up. We persist in prayer, not because we think it
will put pressure on God to grant our request but as
an expression of faith. We continue because we believe
that God's interest in us and in our needs is persistent.
Persistence is evidence of our dependency, not a sign of
our doubt. Another reason we should persist in prayer
is that the needs that prompt those prayers are persistent. Jesus recognized this when he taught the church
to pray for daily bread (Matthew 6:11). The bread that
Jesus teaches us to ask for is a nonrenewable resource.
Once eaten, it will be gone. Yet anyone who has prayed
the Lord's Prayer instinctively senses that the point
of the petition is not terminal but ongoing. We know
that having asked for bread today, we will need to ask
again tomorrow. We grasp that this is the lesson of the
prayer for us. The God who fed us today will also feed
us tomorrow.

Perhaps I am not the mercenary that I thought when it comes to prayer. Jesus did not think of the child who asks for bread as a mercenary. Jesus urged his disciples to persist in prayer with these words: "Which of you, if your son asks for bread, will give him a stone? Or if he asks for a fish, will give him a snake? If you, then, though you are evil, know how to give good gifts to your children, how much more will your Father in heaven give good gifts to those who ask him!" (Matthew 7:9–10). God is not like the reluctant neighbor or the unjust judge in Jesus's parables. It is God's nature to give "good gifts" to his children. God hears us whenever we cry out to him. When God hears, his response is immediate. Although he may not always grant us the particular object of our desire or grant the answer according to our preferred timetable, we can be sure that he will always act in our interest.

Chapter 3

The Art of Praying for Others

Prayer is not a little habit pinned onto us while we were tied to our mother's apron strings; neither is it a little decent quarter of a minute's grace said over an hour's dinner, but it is a most serious work of our most serious years.
—E. M. Bounds

When I was a pastor, one of my responsibilities was to pray for the congregation. I usually began every morning in my "praying chair" with the church directory open on my lap. I would look at the pictures and pray for each person by name. It was easy, as long as I was praying in generalities. It was harder when I tried to pray in specifics. Besides asking God to give them a good day, keep them safe, and bless them (whatever that meant), I often found myself at a loss for words.

My problem wasn't the church's size. The congregation was small, only fifty or sixty regular attenders. I knew everyone by name. I knew where they worked and some of the details of their lives. I was usually aware when something happened worth praying about: an illness, a job change, a death in the family. It wasn't rocket science. It seemed to me that being familiar with the congregation should make praying for them easier, but it wasn't.

Somehow, our proximity made praying more difficult. Maybe the congregation was too familiar. Every day began with the same faces and the same problems. It was tedious. After a while, it was depressing. Nothing seemed to change. *They* never seemed to change. I'm not proud of this but honestly, the daily litany of their weaknesses and troubles was wearying to me. It put me to sleep. Literally.

What Is Intercessory Prayer?

Most of the time, when we pray for others, we are either trying to change them or their situation, but we face two significant obstacles. One is the people for whom we are praying. The other is God. It sometimes seems as if neither party is willing to cooperate with our effort. What does intercessory prayer look like? What should we pray about, and how confident can we be about God's answers to those prayers? Do a search on books about intercessory prayer, and the overall impression you get from the results is that our concerns in this area are primarily questions of focus and method. Many of the titles describe those for whom we should pray. They are about praying for our spouses and children, our nation, and our churches. We are praying for health, prosperity, and revival. These book titles indicate that we wrestle with the same insecurities and disappointments here as we do with the rest of our prayers. We don't think we are very good at it. We are worried about our technique and are looking for some way to ensure we will get the response we desire from God.

The first explicit example of intercessory prayer recorded in Scripture is by Abraham. This doesn't mean that he was the first to pray. People began to "call upon the name of the LORD" in the time of Adam (Genesis 4:26). In part, Abraham's prayers underscore his singular place in God's overall plan. The first prayer that Scripture mentions hardly seems like a prayer at all. It is more like a wish. When Abraham was ninety years old, the Lord made a covenant with him and promised to give him a son by Sarah. The patriarch's knee-jerk reaction was one of incredulity. Genesis 17:17–18: "Abraham fell facedown; he laughed and said to himself, 'Will a son be born to a man a hundred years old? Will Sarah bear a child at the age of ninety?' And Abraham said to God, 'If only Ishmael might live under your blessing!'" Although

Abraham is praised for his faith in Hebrews 11, when he first heard God's promise, it seemed laughable.

There you have it. One sentence blurted out in the heat of the moment. Does it even qualify as a prayer? If it is a prayer, isn't it technically a prayer of disbelief? God told Abraham what he intended to do, and it seemed so unlikely that the patriarch asked God to do the opposite! Abraham's prayer shows us that we are not the first to misunderstand what God is doing. Some of our prayers are merely reactions. We pray them without thinking. They are like reflexes, well-intentioned but misinformed. Like Abraham's request, they usually outline a detailed strategy for God. We know what we want God to do, and we think we know how God should bring it to pass. The nature of our request may even conform generally with God's plan. But God has something else in mind.

The Lord's response to Abraham's thoughtless prayer is unexpected. Instead of being irritated, he brushes Abraham's statement aside with a dismissal that some translations render as "yes, but …" and others translate with "no, but …" Either way, the intent is to assure Abraham of the certainty that the promised child will come through Sarah. Whether Abraham's brief prayer was prompted by a concern that Ishmael might be overlooked or because what God had said seemed too good to be true, this gentle correction should encourage us.

It shows that God sees through the imperfections of our requests to the real intent of our hearts. Our misinformed suggestions or bad advice do not sway him.

Abraham's prayer that the Lord would spare some from the destruction of Sodom is a more typical example of intercessory prayer (Genesis 18:23–33). One of the most surprising features of this prayer is that it sounds like bargaining. It was not Abraham who initiated the conversation but God. The Lord's reason for disclosing his plans was because, "Abraham will surely become a great and powerful nation, and all nations on earth will be blessed through him" (Genesis 18:18). In other words, God invited Abraham to serve as an agent of blessing by interceding for Sodom. The narrative implies that God told Abraham what he was about to do so that the patriarch would intercede.

Abraham did have a personal stake in the outcome. His nephew Lot was a resident of Sodom. Abraham had rescued Lot in the past after Sodom's defeat at the battle of the kings in the Valley of Siddim (Genesis 14:8–12). Now Abraham intervenes again, but this time through prayer. Old Testament scholar Derek Kidner observes, "It would be easy to say that this prayer comes near to haggling, but the right word is 'exploring': Abraham is feeling his way forward in a spirit of faith (superbly expressed in 25c, where he grasps the range and rightness of God's rule), of humility, in his whole mode of address, and of love, demonstrated in his concern for the whole city, not for his kinsmen alone."[1]

The way that Abraham keeps driving down the number of righteous people needed to spare the city of Sodom does indeed make it feel as if he is haggling with a merchant in the marketplace. We sometimes do the same whether we are praying for ourselves or someone else. Our prayers are an attempt to pressure God into operating on our terms. Some may even resort to outright bargaining, offering some commitment or act of devotion in return for God's answer.

Intercession Is not Bargaining

Upon closer inspection, however, clearly there was no bargaining going on at all in Abraham's intercession. A bargain involves an exchange with some quid pro quo given and received. The buyer offers the seller a certain amount in exchange for goods. The leverage in the transaction is that each has something the other wants. Yet Abraham offers nothing in exchange for the terms he suggests to God other than an article of faith. He only asks that "the Judge of all the earth do right" (Genesis 18:25). As for God, he does not negotiate terms with Abraham, but he does acquiesce at each threshold that Abraham proposes. Then he destroys the city anyway (Genesis 19:24–25).

What was the point of this exchange? It proved that God is exactly what Abraham said he was and more. He is a God of justice whose judgment about the moral condition of Sodom was correct. If there had been ten righteous people in the city, the city would have been spared (Genesis 18:32). Instead, God did what Abraham had only implied. He spared Abraham's nephew Lot without being asked.

Abraham also interceded on behalf of Abimelek, king of Gerar. One surprising aspect of this prayer was how Abraham's own actions made it necessary in the first place. While sojourning in Gerar, Abraham told Abimelek, the Philistine king, a half-truth that Sarah was his sister (Genesis 20:2). The patriarch had done this once before when he took up temporary residence in Egypt during a famine. He was motivated by fear, convinced that Sarah's beauty would prompt the Egyptians to kill him so that the Pharaoh could add her to the royal harem (Genesis 12:10–13). Presumably, Abraham was motivated by the same fear in Gerar.

When Abimelek took Sarah into his harem, the Lord came to him in a dream. "You are as good as dead because of the woman you have taken; she is a married woman," he said (Genesis 20:3). Abimelek, who had not yet gone near her, protested: "I have done this with a clear conscience and clean hands" (Genesis 20:4). The Lord agreed and told Abimelek that this was why he had not let the king touch Sarah. "Now return the man's wife, for he is a prophet, and he will pray for you and you will live. But if you do not return her, you may be sure that you and all who belong to you will die" (Genesis 20:7).

Another surprising feature of this account is its absence of explicit criticism for what seems like a clear lapse of faith on Abraham's part. Abraham should have learned from his sojourn in Egypt that God would protect him. Instead, in a strange twist, Abimelek, the "innocent" party, is censured. Maybe the events themselves were reproof enough for Abraham. It hardly seems possible that the irony of the situation was lost on him as he prayed for Abimelek. But the primary purpose of Abraham's intercessory prayer, in this case, seems to have been to single out Abraham as someone that God had marked for a singular destiny. God called Abraham a prophet not because he was a preacher in the formal sense but to underscore the special relationship Abraham enjoyed with God. Abraham was a recipient of divine revelation. God had appeared to Abraham and spoken to him. In this prayer, Abraham stands as God's representative. God granted him the honor of praying for Abimelek not because he had acted honorably but as a matter of grace and calling.

Standing in God's Way

Of all those who pray in the Old Testament, Moses stands as the premier example of intercessory prayer. Two of his most notable prayers occurred when Israel turned from God and worshiped the golden calf (Exodus 32–34) and the rebellion at Kadesh when Israel balked at the prospect of entering the land of Canaan and demanded to return to Egypt (Numbers 13–14). In both cases, Moses's prayer stands between God and the destruction of the nation. In the incident with the golden calf, while Moses was on Mount Sinai, the people of Israel "gathered around Aaron and said, 'Come, make us gods who will go before us'" (Exodus 32:1). Aaron, in turn, demanded that they remove their golden earrings. He used the gold to cast an idol in the shape of a calf and declared, "These are your gods, Israel, who brought you up out of Egypt" (v. 4). Aaron built an altar in front of the calf and announced that the next day would be a festival to Yahweh. After presenting offerings to the calf, "they sat down to eat and drink and got up to indulge in revelry" (v. 6). In other words, even as Moses was receiving the Ten Commandments, God's people were busy breaking the first two, and perhaps the seventh and the tenth as well, if "revelry" has the sexual connotations that many biblical scholars think.[2] When the Lord expressed his intent to destroy the people, Moses "sought the favor" of the Lord (Exodus 32:11).

On the surface, we could be tempted to see this as a momentary flash of rage that subsides after Moses talks God off the ledge. Closer analysis reveals much more. If God had truly wanted to destroy the nation, he could have done so while Moses was still on the mountain. Instead, the Lord said, "Go down, because your people, whom you brought up out of Egypt, have become corrupt" (Exodus 32:7). More than informing Moses of the problem, this declaration is cleverly framed in a way that seems to place their fate in Moses's hands. In addition to calling them "your people, whom you brought up out of Egypt," the Lord demands, "Now leave me alone so that my anger may burn against them and that I may destroy them. Then I will make you into a great nation" (v. 10). In the exchange that follows, Moses prays four times and offers three arguments based on what God has already revealed about his purpose and character.

The first argument is an appeal to God's past actions and promises. Moses argued that destroying them would give the Egyptians occasion to slander God. These were not Moses's people but God's, fulfilling his promise to Abraham, Isaac, and Jacob (Exodus 32:11–13). Moses's second argument took place after Moses dashed the two tablets against the foot of the mountain and took steps to punish those who had not obeyed. Moses went back to the Lord and admitted that the people had committed a great wickedness. He pleaded with God to forgive them, including a bold ultimatum: "But now, please forgive their sin—but if not, then blot me out of the book you have written" (Exodus 32:32). The Lord refused and struck the people with a plague.

Moses's third exchange with God, also his most intense, came after the Lord ordered the Israelites to break camp and resume their journey without his immediate presence. He promised to send an angel before them to drive out their enemies but refused to go with them himself "because you are a stiff-necked people and I might destroy you on the way" (Exodus 33:3). Not only did Moses ask for God's continued presence, but he also made a bold personal request in Exodus 33:18: "Now show me your glory." What followed was a glorious vision of God as he receded from view (Exodus 33:23). There must have been a visual element to this encounter, yet what is recorded is not a description of what Moses saw but an affirmation of God's gracious and compassionate nature. He is slow to anger and abounds in love and faithfulness, but he does not leave the guilty unpunished (Exodus 34:6–7). This view of God gives Moses the confidence to intercede a fourth time and ask God to go with them (Exodus 34:9).

Moses's prayer for Israel at Kadesh has similar features. However, at Kadesh, his intercession was not because of idolatry but a rebellion that sprang from Israel's lack of faith. As the assembly discussed stoning Moses and Aaron, the glory of God appeared over the tent of meeting, and the Lord threatened to destroy them: "I will strike them down with a plague and destroy them, but I will make you into a nation greater and stronger than they" (Numbers 14:12). As in his earlier prayer, Moses argued that such an action would cause the Egyptians to draw the wrong conclusions about God's power. This time, however, he prayed back to God the attributes that were revealed to Moses when he saw God's glory. "The LORD is slow to anger, abounding in love and forgiving sin and rebellion. Yet he does not leave the guilty unpunished; he punishes the children for the sin of the parents to the third and fourth generation," Moses prayed. "In accordance with your great love, forgive the sin of these people, just as you have pardoned them from the time they left Egypt until now" (Numbers 14:18–19).

These examples capture the essence of intercessory prayer. It is not bargaining or talking God into or out of something. When we pray for others, we respond to God's invitation to enter into his purposes. Instead of carefully crafted arguments intended to persuade a reluctant God, we confess God's promises. His grace, mercy, and justice shape our petitions. The more we know about God, the more confidently and intelligently we can pray.

Participatory Praying

When I was a pastor, I was surprised at how frequently people asked me to pray for them, as if my prayers carried more weight with God than their own. But when I thought about it, I realized that I had often done the same. Down through the ages, God's people have always asked their spiritual leaders to pray for them. These leaders, in turn, saw this as a duty. The prophet Samuel is a good example. When the Israelites realized the gravity of what they had done by demanding that Samuel place a king over them, they begged God's prophet to pray for them. Samuel responded by urging them not to turn away from the Lord but to serve him with all their heart. Then he added this assurance: "As for me, far be it from me that I should sin against the LORD by failing to pray for you. And I will teach you the way that is good and right" (1 Samuel 12:23).

The New Testament apostles thought similarly. When the church's numerical growth caused some of the church's widows to be overlooked in the daily distribution of food, Peter responded: "Brothers and sisters, choose seven men from among you who are known to be full of the Spirit and wisdom. We will turn this responsibility over to them and will give our attention to prayer and the ministry of the word" (Acts 6:4). This was not a dismissal of the problem. They recognized the importance of this congregational concern and realized that it would demand a level of attention that would cause them to neglect their own ministry priorities. It is noteworthy that among those priorities, Peter gives intercessory prayer first place.

But if the church leaders are supposed to pray for the flock, who prays for the leader? The church leaders are not the only ones who engage in intercessory prayer. The church does not have an official class of people who pray. As a royal priesthood, every believer enjoys the privilege of interceding for others (1 Peter 2:5, 9; Revelation 1:6; 5:10). The church leaders benefit when the congregation prays for them. The apostle Paul often urged the church to pray for him and his ministry. "Devote yourselves to prayer, being watchful and thankful," he urged the Colossians. "And pray for us, too, that God may open a door for our message, so that we may proclaim the mystery of Christ, for which I am in chains" (Colossians 4:3). Paul was convinced that the church's prayers would result in new opportunities for him to share the mystery of Christ. He believed that their prayers had an effect on his circumstances.

In Romans 15:30, Paul describes prayer as a struggle: "I urge you, brothers and sisters, by our Lord Jesus Christ and by the love of the Spirit, to join me in my struggle by praying to God for me." Some see an echo of Jacob's wrestling match with the angel of the Lord in these words (Genesis 32:24–32; cf. Colossians 4:12). But the language of *shared* struggle suggests that Paul probably has something else in view. New Testament commentator C. E. B. Cranfield concludes: "what Paul is entreating them to do is simply to pray for him and with him, not half-heartedly or casually, but with earnestness, urgency and persistency."[3] Paul employs a simpler form of the word translated "struggle with" elsewhere to speak of struggles associated with his ministry (Philippians 1:30; Colossians 2:1; 1 Thessalonians 2:2). The language of Romans 15:30 also suggests that those who prayed for Paul not only joined the apostle in prayer but shared in his ministry. We do more than deliver someone else's grocery list of needs to God when we pray for them. One of the reasons intercessory prayer can seem tedious is because it feels redundant. Those for whom we pray are making the same requests that we are. God knows what everyone is going to say before they say it. Since he understands the need better than us, the whole thing feels a little unnecessary. We wonder whether our voice adds any value. It is easy to see ourselves as spiritual bureaucrats who are merely sending others' requests up the chain of command.

But the vocabulary of shared experience in Romans 15:30 seems to imply that intercessory prayer is much more than this. It is participatory language. Intercessory prayer is not just a formality. It is more than an empty ritual, where we go through the motions of reciting words like spiritual functionaries in the court of heaven, and God does what he was going to do anyway. Praying for someone is a way to enter into their experience from a distance. When we pray for others, we join their efforts. Prayer is relational on another level. When we pray for others, we approach God on their behalf. This God, as Scripture reveals, is a unity of three persons who are in fellowship with one another and who are involved with those for whom we pray. When we engage in intercessory prayer, we are not trying to direct God's attention toward someone he is not aware of or in whom he is not interested. When we pray for someone else, we enter into a relationship that already exists between that person and God as their creator.

Paul's language of spiritual collaboration places intercessory prayer within a relational rather than a transactional framework. In 1 Corinthians 3:9, the apostle says that he and Apollos are God's "co-workers." Likewise, Paul also saw the Corinthians as his helpers through their prayers. Those who prayed for Paul enabled him to preach. Their prayers went on ahead and opened doors.

The same is true for us. When we pray for a friend going through a hard time, we share the load with them. Our prayers can ease their burden. In 2 Corinthians 1:8, Paul writes that when he was in the province of Asia, he faced troubles "far beyond our ability to endure, so that we despaired of life itself." Although he did not reveal the exact nature of the difficulties he faced, he said that they seemed like a death sentence at the time (v. 9). The apostle goes on to assure the Corinthians: "He has delivered us from such a deadly peril, and he will deliver us again. On him we have set our hope that he will continue to deliver us, as you help us by your prayers. Then many will give thanks on our behalf for the gracious favor granted us in answer to the prayers of many" (vv. 10–11). The prayers of believers helped Paul when he despaired of life. God granted the deliverance, but he did so "in answer to the prayers of many."

The record of Paul's prayers in his letters and his requests that the churches pray for him in return provide evidence of a praying network that was the foundation of the apostle's ministry. Paul not only solicited prayers for himself but invited them to pray along with him for others. "Thus the ministry of letter-writing and reading would be deepened by a reciprocal priestly ministry of intercessory supplications," Gordon Wiles explains, "while they responded to his further invitation that they in turn pray for him."[4]

To say that prayer is participatory in nature does not deny the fact that the act of praying can itself be a struggle. We do people a disservice when we talk about prayer as if it were easy. According to a common saying, often heard at mission conferences, "a few can go, some can give, but all can pray." Those who say this speak as if prayer were the lowest form of Christian service. It is the sort of thing that anyone can do. They seem to imply that prayer is an easy task that requires little skill or effort.

The nineteenth-century Anglican bishop J. C. Ryle wrote:

> It is useless to say you do not know how to pray. Prayer is the simplest act in all religion. It is simply speaking to God. It needs neither learning, nor wisdom, nor book-knowledge to begin it. It needs nothing but heart and will. The weakest infant can cry when he is hungry. The poorest beggar can hold out his hand for alms, and does not wait to find words. The most ignorant man will find something to say to God, if he has only a mind.[5]

Ryle is correct when he observes that prayer is simple. What could be simpler than to open your mouth and speak? But simple does not necessarily mean easy. If prayer is a way to participate in the ministry of others and share their struggles, we should not be surprised to find that it is also arduous at times. In Colossians 4:12, Paul uses athletic imagery when he says of Epaphras: "He is always wrestling in prayer for you, that you may stand firm in all the will of God, mature and fully assured." Intercessory prayer demands the same kind of effort required of the athlete. It calls for initiative, discipline, and persistence.

However, it would be a mistake to think that all intercessory prayer requires is a little effort on our part. In Romans 15:30, Paul urged his readers "by our Lord Jesus Christ and by the love of the Spirit" to pray for him. Love is a primary motive for intercessory prayer. By connecting love with the Spirit, Paul traces this love ultimately back to God. We pray for others because we care about them. We care about them because God has given us the capacity to care. In this way, our prayers become an extension of God's love for others.

Another thing that energizes our prayers is the conviction that our prayers will have an effect. As Paul puts it in 2 Corinthians 1:11, prayer *helps*. Prayers offered on behalf of others provide practical help. When we pray for someone in need, our prayers are part of the process that God uses to meet that need. In a sense, God allows us to bring what they need to them through our prayers. Some have difficulty reconciling this with what the Bible teaches about God's sovereignty. To say that the prayers of believers opened doors for the apostle that would not otherwise have opened seems to infringe on God's power. Paul, however, had no such qualms. He attributed his deliverance to God but also recognized that God had used others' prayers as a means. If prayer changes things, those changes were anticipated by God. Not only were they anticipated, but they were also initiated by him as well.

The seeming conflict between the effect of our praying and the sovereignty of God is a false one. It assumes that prayer's effect comes because we invite God into our plans. Such thinking mistakenly assumes that God's answer is only a response to our initiative. It is the other way around. When we pray, we do not invite God into our plans. Instead, he uses prayer to draw us into his. There is indeed a mystery here but no more than in any of the things that we do. The infinite God seems to delight in working through finite agents to accomplish his purposes. We pray for healing and go to the doctor. We ask God to provide our daily bread and go to work to earn money to buy food from the grocery store. The one who plants also prays. "It is not really stranger, nor less strange, that my prayers should affect the course of events than that my other actions should do so," C. S. Lewis observes. "They have not advised or changed

God's mind—that is His over-all purpose. But that purpose will be realized in different ways according to the actions, including the prayers, of His creatures."[6]

Although we would like to understand how divine sovereignty, omniscience, and omnipotence work together with human freedom and individual initiative in prayer, we do not need to know in order to pray. Nor do we need to know why a good God, who is already aware of what is needed, would make his answers contingent upon our asking. We may puzzle over these questions, but we do not need to answer them to pray. It is enough to know that God is good and that he has invited us to bring our concerns to him. If the prayers that we pray for others have a real effect on their lives and circumstances, why would we refuse to pray simply because we do not understand why God has chosen to work in this way? The knowledge that praying *does* help is all we really need to know.

How to Pray for Others

How, then, should we practice the art of intercessory prayer? To some extent, the answer is that intercessory prayer is the same as any other kind of praying. We bring our concerns to God and ask him to take care of them. The apostle Paul's prayers recorded in the New Testament provide a simple model that we can use for ourselves. Many of his prayers include four key elements.[7] First, they are addressed to God. But rather than merely saying, "Dear God," Paul's openings often describe God by one of his attributes as recorded in Scripture. The prayer in Romans 15:5 begins, "May the God who gives endurance and encouragement give you the same attitude of mind toward each other that Christ Jesus had." The brief benedictory prayer of Romans 15:33 is addressed to "the God of peace" (see also Romans 16:20). The prayer of praise in 2 Corinthians 1:3 describes God as "the God and Father of our Lord Jesus Christ, the Father of compassion and the God of all comfort."

The second element of Paul's prayers is the request itself. Sometimes these are stated explicitly as petitions and at other times in words that sound more like a wish. Paul's use of the optative mood does not mean that he was uncertain of getting an answer. This is simply the language of desire. For example, in 1 Thessalonians 5:23 Paul prays, "May God himself, the God of peace, sanctify you through and through. May your whole spirit, soul and body be kept blameless at the coming of our Lord Jesus Christ." This wish is followed by a promise, "The one who calls you is faithful, and he will do it" (v. 24).

The point here is not so much whether we use the optative mood or the indicative when we make our requests so much as it is that we see those for whom we pray within the framework of God's care. We are not merely asking for things. We are making our requests with a Godward focus. Petitions framed in the optative recognize that a petition is not a demand. It is language that respects God's right to refuse our requests for his own reasons. When we express our requests in the indicative, we acknowledge that we are speaking to the God of promise who is faithful and will keep his word. We can come to him in confidence. Although we may not always know exactly how God will answer our prayer, we can be sure that he *will* answer. Our prayers may feel like wishes, but they are more than this. We can make our requests with the confidence of knowing that they are addressed to one who is faithful and can do what we ask.

The third feature of Paul's prayers is that they usually mention those for whom he prays. He has specific people in mind. Paul's prayers for others are personal and suited to their needs. They are not vague. Sometimes the nature of what Paul requests is determined by their situation. At other times, the content of his prayers is shaped by God's promises. These are a helpful guide when we feel like we don't know how to pray for others. Begin by thinking about their circumstances. What needs do you already know about? Have they expressed concerns to you? If you don't feel like you have enough information to be specific, you can always base your prayers on God's promises in Scripture. The recorded prayers of others can serve as a guide. Passages like Ephesians 1:17–19, 3:16–21, Philippians 1:9–11, Colossians 1:9–12, Philemon 4–6, 3 John 2, or even Aaron's priestly benediction in Numbers 6:24–26 offer many ideas of how you can pray for others. When you think about it, any legitimate Scripture promise can be turned into a prayer for someone else.

A fourth element of the apostle's prayers is that Paul often articulates an outcome that he expects to see as a result of God's answer. In Ephesians 1:17–19, he prayed that God would grant the Ephesian believers "the Spirit of revelation and wisdom" so that they would "know him better." In this prayer he also asked God to enlighten their hearts so that they would "know the hope" to which they had been called. In Colossians 1:9–12, Paul asks God to fill the Colossians with "the knowledge of his will through all the wisdom and understanding that the Spirit gives," so that they might "live a life worthy of the Lord and please him in every way: bearing fruit in every good work, growing in the knowledge of God." He also prayed that they might be "strengthened with all power according to his glorious might," so that they would "have great endurance and patience, and giving joyful thanks to the Father," who qualified them, "to share in the inheritance of his holy people in the kingdom of light." Then, as if this weren't enough, in verses 13 and 14, the apostle goes on to give the reason he feels confident to pray this for them: "For he has rescued us from the dominion of darkness and brought us into the kingdom of the Son he loves, in whom we have redemption, the forgiveness of sins."

These purpose clauses set the apostle's requests within the larger framework of God's plan. It is easy to be so caught up in the specific requests we are making that we lose sight of why we are praying at all. Christian prayer is not magic. We are not trying to conjure things by speaking the right words to God. We are participating in God's plan for the church, for our lives, and the world at large. There is a bigger picture to keep in view, along with the particular requests that we make. God's purposes and his promises are a motivator and a guide in all our praying.

There is one other noteworthy feature of Paul's intercessory prayers. Those that are recorded in the New Testament are generally brief. Often, they are no more than a paragraph or two. Many are only a few sentences. This brevity does not fit the image we usually have of what intercessory prayer looks like. We imagine someone who spends hours on their knees. We think of a monk in his cell, a godly widow who spends hours alone in her home, or a bedfast invalid who ranges far and wide in their prayer life.

The church's history does include many remarkable examples of prayer. According to the church historian Eusebius, James of Jerusalem, the brother of Jesus who was also called James the Just, spent so much time in prayer that "his knees grew hard like a camel's because of his constant worship of God, kneeling and asking forgiveness for the people."[8] John Hyde, the nineteenth-century missionary to India, was known to spend so many hours pleading with God for revival that he was nicknamed Praying Hyde. Peggy and Christine Smith, two sisters in their eighties who lived on the Scottish Isle of Barvas in the 1950s and whose arthritis would not permit them to attend church, prayed night and day for revival. They were instrumental in inviting the evangelist Duncan Campbell, whose preaching sparked the Hebrides revival.

Some believers seem to have a special gift for prayer. They are themselves a gift to the church. Yet their example, as inspiring as it is, may also leave ordinary people feeling that intercessory prayer is beyond them. It belongs to the spiritual elite. We must work and care for our families. We do not have the luxury of devoting night and day exclusively to prayer for others. Aside from the natural hindrance posed by the limits of our attention span, we wouldn't know how to spend the time anyway. We are asking God to provide them with healing or work or help in their relationships. Our requests are usually not so complicated that we cannot state them in a few sentences. Jesus has already warned us that we cannot pressure God by piling up words when we pray (Matthew 6:7).

We also seem to forget that many of the prayers that Paul recorded in his letters are not executive summaries of longer prayers prayed at an earlier time. They are actual prayers. In other words, Paul seemed to have no problem doing two things at once. He could pray *and* write. Perhaps this is the way we should understand his admonition in 1 Thessalonians 5:17 that believers should "pray continually." We do not need to be spiritual professionals or confined to the house to engage in intercessory prayer. We can pray while we work or drive or make dinner. Our prayers do not have to be monologues. A sentence or two is enough to be heard by God.

It seems that Bishop Ryle was right after all. It does not take much to pray for ourselves or others. All we need is a mind to pray. Our prayers do not have to be works of art. They do not have to be long. We can pray while working, playing, or as we lie on our bed at night. Say what you have to say as best you can and leave the matter with God. Do not be discouraged if your mind wanders. If you haven't finished expressing yourself, finish your thought and move on to whatever you must do next. If you happen to doze off, don't beat yourself up. Perhaps you needed the rest. Scripture says, "He grants sleep to those he loves" (Psalm 127:2).

Chapter 4

Managing Our Angry Prayers

Yank some of the groans out of your prayers,
and shove in some shouts.
—Billy Sunday

Sometimes I pray because I am angry with other people. On other occasions, I pray because I am angry with God. When Jonah prayed, it was both.

After delivering what may be the shortest and most successful sermon in preaching history, Jonah prayed an angry prayer in which he took God to task for his mercy and then begged to die. This was after Jonah's ill-advised attempt to hire a ship to flee to Tarshish and the raging storm and after being tossed over the side of the boat and then vomited back onto dry land after three days. Despite his false start, God's prophet completed his mission with such success that everyone in the city of Nineveh repented. Even the animals had repented, after a fashion (Jonah 3:6–9). Instead of destroying the city, as Jonah had warned, God "relented and did not bring on them the destruction he had threatened" (Jonah 3:10). You might think that Jonah would be happy. Instead, the prophet was outraged. The Hebrew text literally says, "It was evil to Jonah, a great evil and he was angry" (Jonah 4:1).

Jonah wasn't surprised by what God had done (or, more specifically, by what he *hadn't* done). Jonah was furious because God had behaved exactly as he expected. "Isn't this what I said, LORD, when I was still at home?" he complained in Jonah 4:2–3. "That is what I tried to forestall by fleeing to Tarshish. I knew that you are a gracious and compassionate God, slow to anger and abounding in love, a God who relents from sending calamity. Now, LORD, take away my life, for it is better for me to die than to live." In the belly of the fish, Jonah's prayers were full of praise and quotes from the Psalms. Now all he wanted to do was die.

God answered Jonah with a terse question: "Is it right for you to be angry?" The prophet's response was framed in actions instead of words. He stationed himself east of the city, built a little shelter to protect himself from the heat, and then sat down to wait for the fire to fall from heaven and destroy Nineveh like Sodom and Gomorrah. Instead, the only heat that Jonah felt came from the sun's burning rays. When God caused a plant to spring up with leaves to shade him, Jonah was "very happy about the plant" (Jonah 4:6). No doubt, he was happy because of the shade it provided. But it is likely that he was happier yet because Jonah took the vine's sudden appearance as a sign that God had begun to see the matter his way. That joy only lasted about a day. With the coming of the next dawn, a plant-eating worm appeared and caused the plant to wither. As dawn was breaking, it brought a scorching east wind. The sun once again beat down upon him, and the prophet renewed his angry petition. "It would be better for me to die than to live," he said.

God's response this time was a version of his earlier question: "Is it right for you to be angry about the plant?" Jonah did not hesitate to answer. "It is," he said. "And I'm so angry I wish I were dead" (Jonah 4:9). But instead of granting Jonah his request, the Lord, who is a gracious and compassionate God, slow to anger and abounding in love, and a God who relents from sending calamity, tried to reason with his angry prophet. "You have been concerned about this plant, though you did not tend it or make it grow. It sprang up overnight and died overnight," God said to him. "And should I not have concern for the great city of Nineveh, in which there are more than a hundred and twenty thousand people who cannot tell their right hand from their left—and also many animals?" (Jonah 4:10).

We are inclined to dismiss Jonah's angry prayers as an aberration. He seems to us to be a petulant and spoiled prophet, a primitive man who clings to the old code of *lex talionis* (a Latin phrase meaning "law of the tooth") and refuses to embrace God's mercy. We, who like to think of ourselves as children of a more enlightened age, are embarrassed to find him in the company of the prophets.

Yet, Jonah's angry prayers are not an anomaly. Indeed, angry prayers are common enough that those who study the prayers of the Bible have an entire category devoted to them. They call them *imprecatory* prayers, after a Latin word that means to curse or invoke evil. To be fair, Jonah's prayers were not technically imprecatory. They were more occasions of grumbling out loud to God. But the anger that prompted them is the same spirit that fuels the imprecations of the Psalms, the laments of Jeremiah, and even a few of the "wish prayers" of the apostle Paul (Galatians 1:8; 5:12). "Judging from the psalms of lament," Michael Widmer observes, "a wide-spread prayer practice in ancient Israel was the invocation of divine justice and retribution (e.g. Pss 69, 74, 79). There are more than 40 imprecatory petitions in the Psalter alone."[1]

Cry for Justice

Prayers for protection have always been prayed by God's people. Jacob prayed, "Save me, I pray, from the hand of my brother Esau, for I am afraid he will come and attack me, and also the mothers with their children" (Genesis 32:11). Jabez asked God to enlarge his territory and keep him from pain (1 Chronicles 4:10). The early church asked the Lord to consider those rulers' threats who had conspired against Christ and grant them boldness to proclaim the gospel (Acts 4:29).

Imprecatory prayers go a step further. They ask for protection, but they also ask God to punish, sometimes with language that we would consider immoderate. For example, in Psalm 69:28, David prays that God would blot his enemies out of the book of life. Even more disturbing, Psalm 137:8–9 pronounces a curse on Babylon and a blessing on those who destroy it: "Daughter Babylon, doomed to destruction, happy is the one who repays you according to what you have done to us. Happy is the one who seizes your infants and dashes them against the rocks." The prophet Jeremiah, who witnessed the Babylonian atrocities the psalmist laments, often complains to God and calls upon him to take vengeance. In Jeremiah 18:21, the prophet asks God to "give their children over to famine; hand them over to the power of the sword. Let their wives be made childless and widows; let their men be put to death, their young men slain by the sword in battle."

Anyone who has experienced abuse or witnessed an atrocity can identify with the emotion that energizes

these prayers. But we don't have to suffer abuse to understand the angry prayers of the Psalms and prophets. We
have all had the same feelings, though on a much smaller
scale, every time someone has wronged us. Yet, there is
more than an emotion behind the imprecations of the
Old Testament. The retributive standard of the Mosaic
law—eye for an eye, tooth for tooth, hand for hand, foot
for foot—shapes them. Leviticus 24:20 summarizes the
principle in these words: "The one who has inflicted
the injury must suffer the same injury" (see also Exodus
21:24; Deuteronomy 19:21).

As a legal standard, this guideline set the bounds for
those who bore the responsibility of determining punishment. Its purpose was to limit retribution. The basic
rule of *lex talionis* was that the punishment should fit the
crime and not go beyond it. Any penalty must consider
the degree of damage inflicted on the victim and the
retaliation imposed should not have extreme punitive
damages. This was often the case in the ancient world.
For example, when Shechem raped Jacob's daughter
Dinah, his sons Simeon and Levi killed Shechem, his
father, and every man in the city. Then, the rest of Jacob's
sons looted the city. Genesis 34:29 says, "They carried
off all their wealth and all their women and children,
taking as plunder everything in the houses." In our day,

we would probably decry this as a revenge killing. But it was a fairly common practice in the ancient Near East.

The Mosaic law's limitation of the penalty to an eye for an eye and a tooth for a tooth was not exclusive to Israel. It existed in other cultures as well, perhaps most famously in the Babylonian Code of Hammurabi. Possibly we might view the psalmist's and Jeremiah's imprecatory prayers as an application of the Babylonians' own standard of law against them, but the limits set by God's law on retribution were more than a cultural adaption of advanced Babylonian jurisprudence. It reflected a larger movement in the direction of grace that Jesus Christ would eventually fulfill by his coming. John gives the broad outline of this trajectory when he observes that "the law was given through Moses; grace and truth came through Jesus Christ" (John 1:17).

Surely John does not mean that grace and truth were entirely absent from the law. In Psalm 119:142 the psalmist declares, "Your righteousness is everlasting and your law is true." The limiting nature of the eye-for-eye principle in the Mosaic law was itself a reflection of God's grace, as was the law's overall message. The law's system of offerings and sacrifices showed the need for grace and pointed forward to the once-for-all offering of Christ, making the grace in the law dependent upon Christ. The forgiveness offered in the law did not come from the law itself but from Christ's sacrifice: "For this reason Christ is the mediator of a new covenant, that those who are called may receive the promised eternal inheritance—now that he has died as a ransom to set them free from the sins committed under the first covenant" (Hebrews 9:15). Christ's coming has effected a change, described by John as the arrival of grace and truth. In this way, Jesus completed the trajectory of grace anticipated by the Old Testament.

Christ's inauguration of this full measure of grace must shape our understanding of Scripture's angry prayers. The advent of an age of grace did not lower the bar of God's justice. Jesus did not come to overturn the law but to fulfill it (Matthew 5:17–18). Not only did Jesus warn of a coming day of judgment, but he also made it clear that on that day, he would be its primary agent (Matthew 13:41–43; cf. 2 Peter 2:9; 3:7). But until that day, Christ's dealings with the offender are marked by grace.

As the time drew near for his crucifixion, Jesus set out for Jerusalem to meet it head-on. During the journey, he sent messengers ahead to a Samaritan village that lay along the route to arrange for hospitality. But when the residents learned where Jesus was headed, they refused to welcome him (Luke 9:51–53). This refusal was prompted by long-standing hostility between Jews and Samaritans about the proper place to worship. Jews worshiped at the temple in Jerusalem while the Samaritans believed that Mount Gerizim was the proper place (see John 4:20). The Samaritans thought of themselves as worshipers of the same God as the Jews, but the Jews viewed them as foreigners and heretics. The antipathy between the two lasted for hundreds of years. It was so strong that several Samaritans defiled the temple by scattering bones there sometime between AD 9–10.

In addition to its religious implications (the Samaritans' refusal to welcome Jesus amounted to a rejection of his messianic claim), their unwillingness to grant hospitality would have been seen both as a social insult and a moral offense. The Mosaic law condemned the Ammonites and Moabites for refusing to extend hospitality to Israel during their wilderness journey (Deuteronomy 23:3–4). This background enables us to better understand why James and John responded with such anger when the Samaritan village turned Jesus away; they offered to call down fire from heaven and destroy them. Instead of laughing off their suggestion, which was not meant as a joke but made in deadly earnest, Jesus turned and rebuked them (Luke 9:54–55).

The Spirit of Grace

The spirit that shapes our prayers for those who anger us is not the spirit of Jonah (or James and John) but the spirit of Christ. It is not a cry for justice but a prayer for grace.

To hear such a thing will undoubtedly rankle some in this era when justice has become a cultural byword. Yet Jesus could not have been clearer on this matter in his teaching. Our model is not the imprecatory prayers of the Psalms and prophets, but the pattern Christ gave us in the Sermon on the Mount. "You have heard that it was said, 'Love your neighbor and hate your enemy,'" Jesus declared. "But I tell you, love your enemies and pray for those who persecute you, that you may be children of your Father in heaven. He causes his sun to rise on the evil and the good, and sends rain on the righteous and the unrighteous" (Matthew 5:43–45). But what kind of prayer shall we pray for those we judge to be our persecutors? Paul echoes Christ's command and clarifies the sort of prayer he had in mind: "Bless those who persecute you; bless and do not curse" (Romans 12:15).

If Jesus's teaching about prayer for those who persecute us is hard to accept, the instructions that set the stage for it in Matthew 5:38–42 are even harder to swallow. In this section of the sermon, Jesus takes direct aim at the principle of *lex talionis* and eliminates it as an option for the individual disciple:

> You have heard that it was said, "Eye for eye, and tooth for tooth." But I tell you, do not resist an evil person. If anyone slaps you on the right cheek, turn to them the other cheek also. And if anyone wants to sue you and take your shirt, hand over your coat as well. If anyone forces you to go one mile, go with them two miles. Give to the one who asks you, and do not turn away from the one who wants to borrow from you.

Indeed, even in the Mosaic law, it was never the individual's right to exact vengeance according to the standard of *lex talionis*. The rule of "eye for eye" provided guidance for those whose responsibility it was to judge. "What Jesus affirmed in the antithesis was rather that this principle, though it pertains to the law courts and the judgment of God, is not applicable to our personal relationships," John Stott explains. "These are to be based on love, not justice."[2]

Does this mean that God has no interest in seeing that justice is done or that we should be cavalier about injustice? Not at all.

Praying, as Jesus teaches us to pray, does not mean that we need to try and hide the fact that we are angry.

Nor do we need to ignore the evil that has been done.
We do not need to deny that we would like to see God
put things right. The Bible's angry prayers prove that outrage is a common emotion among the godly. These angry
prayers express a longing like that of the Old Testament
patriarch Lot, who 2 Peter 2:8 says, "was tormented in
his righteous soul by the lawless deeds he saw and heard."
The fact that Scripture repeatedly reminds us that the
right of retribution ultimately belongs to God alone is
proof that the desire to see the wicked punished is uni-
versal (Deuteronomy 32:35; Psalm 94:1; Romans 12:19;
Hebrews 10:30). Even those who dwell in heaven express
this longing (Revelation 6:9–10). God's answer to them
is the same one that he offers to us: "Wait a little longer."

Why should we be patient? There are three crucial
reasons for not giving ourselves over to the anger we feel,
even when we are justifiably angry. First, as Scripture
repeatedly affirms, the day of reckoning for which we
pray will come in its own time. All of Scripture, especially Jesus's own teaching, is clear that everyone will
one day give an account to God for the things they have
done. God is not finished with evil.

Second, the work that God is doing in the inter-
vening time is the work of salvation. By demanding
an immediate reckoning, we would deny to others the
same salvation that Christ has granted to us. A day of

reckoning is coming, but this is not that day. When we are angry, we long for the day of justice, but "now is the time of God's favor, now is the day of salvation" (2 Corinthians 6:2). If we could hasten judgment, we would cut short God's primary work, which is salvation. Like the servants in Jesus's parable, if God were to grant our desire, it would likely uproot the wheat along with the weeds (Matthew 13:24–30).

Third, our anger may blind us to the patience God has displayed toward us. Here is the real threat: that our eagerness to see others held accountable will blind us to the grace that God has shown to us. We may easily forget that we, too, were once deserving of God's judgment. We may act as if the righteous standing we now enjoy in Christ was our own instead of coming to us as a gift. This is why the Savior warned his disciples about the danger of judging others. When Jesus said, "Do not judge, or you too will be judged," in Matthew 7:1, Jesus was not saying that it is wrong to have moral standards. He was not even saying that it is wrong to draw conclusions about the moral quality of another person's behavior. Verse 2 clarifies the danger: "For in the same way you judge others, you will be judged, and with the measure you use, it will be measured to you."

How do we reconcile this with our obligation to "act justly" (Micah 6:8)? A desire for justice is legitimate. We have a responsibility to protect the interests of those in need when it is within our power to do so. Scripture calls for both prayer and action. But there is a danger that we will be too one-sided in our passion for justice. We may demand that the letter of the law be applied to others while expecting a pass for ourselves. We may also be so fixed on justice that we forget our corollary obligation to show mercy. In this age of social media, it is far too easy to think of outrage as synonymous with justice. Prayer, however, is a way of expressing our longing for justice that goes beyond venting. When we pray for justice, we invite God to intervene in the situation. Prayer is itself a form of social action. Yet Micah 6:8 calls us to "act justly" *and* "love mercy." As we call upon God for his justice and pray for our enemies as Jesus both taught and modeled, we keep these two obligations in balance.

If we demand that the standard of *lex talionis* be applied to others, we are in effect inviting God to deal with us according to the same measure. We may be right to say that others have done wrong. Our assessment of the grievous harm they have done to us may be accurate. We are even correct in thinking that the evil they have done deserves to be punished measure for measure. What we are forgetting is that, in our case, someone else took the punishment for us: "We all, like sheep, have gone astray, each of us has turned to our own way; and the LORD has laid on him the iniquity of us all" (Isaiah 53:6).

When Jesus told the parable of the Good Samaritan, it prompted the question, "Who is my neighbor?" (Luke 10:29). Given Jesus's command that we must love our enemies and pray for those who persecute us, we might ask a different question. Who is my *enemy*? There are many places in the world where the church suffers violent persecution. In recent years, the erosion of liberties has sparked fear in countries where freedom of religion was once a core value. Yet if asked what has prompted our angry prayers, most of us would say, "The wounds I was given at the house of my friends" (Zechariah 13:6). It is not only our persecutors who have hurt us but those in our family, our workplace, and, often, in our church. It is no accident that it was the church that the apostle Paul said must "bear with each other and forgive one another if any of you has a grievance against someone. Forgive as the Lord forgave you" (Colossians 3:13). If we ask, "Who is my neighbor?" or "Who is my enemy?" the answer is often the same.

How to Pray through Anger

How, then, should we pray our angry prayers? Given what Jesus says, should we even pray them at all? It does not seem realistic to think that we can deny our anger.

To deny it would be to pray through a mask of false piety. We cannot hide our feelings from the one that Scripture says "knew what was in each person" (John 2:24). Nor is it reasonable to dismiss the things that have sparked our outrage. They are important. At least, they are important to us, or else we would not be angry about them. Whether or not the outrage we feel is justified is not the point (not yet anyway). If we are to worship God in spirit and truth, the truest self at this moment is our angry self. Jesus's command to love our enemy and bless our persecutors does not mean that we cannot pray if we are angry. "My hunch is that there is a way *beyond* the Psalms of vengeance, but it is a way *through* them and not *around* them," Walter Brueggemann notes.[3] The imprecatory psalms testify to the reality of God's vengeance. They also bear witness to the fact that we are vengeful creatures by nature. "Our rage and indignation must be fully owned and fully expressed," Brueggemann explains. "And then (only then) can our rage and indignation be *yielded* to the mercy of God."[4]

We do not have to deny our anger, but we must take these feelings in hand and discipline ourselves to pray both as Jesus taught us and as he himself prayed. In his second epistle, Peter assures his readers that there will be an accounting. On the day of judgment, those who have refused to accept God's grace through Christ will

bear the full weight of *lex talionis* when they are called
to account for their actions. They "will be paid back with
harm for the harm they have done" (2 Peter 2:13). We
are given this reassurance not so that we will take plea-
sure in their perdition but so that we will trust God to
do what is right.

Nevertheless, if we are to pray as Jesus did, then we
must take upon our lips not only his words of forgiveness
offered on behalf of those who crucified him but his cry
of dereliction. Before Jesus prayed, "Father, forgive them,"
he prayed, "My God, my God, why have you forsaken
me?" (Matthew 27:46; Mark 15:34). I am not saying that
on the cross, Jesus spoke in anger or disappointment
with the Father. Far from it. Indeed, by claiming the
words of Psalm 22:1 as his own, Jesus claimed the psalm's
promise of vindication (Psalm 22:22–31).

Yet these words of anguish were more than a mere
symbol. Just as they truly described the emotion of the
psalmist at the time when they were first written, they
express the agony Christ suffered as he "'bore our sins' in
his body on the cross" (1 Peter 2:24). This was an agony
that moved him to pray in the Garden of Gethsemane
until he sweat drops of blood (Luke 22:44). The prospect
of such suffering compelled him to ask three times to be
spared the cup of suffering. This was an honest admission
by Jesus of what he characterized as a "will" or "desire"

that somehow differed from the Father's without being an act of disobedience. What kept it from being a sin was Christ's overarching submission. Although his human desire was to avoid the cup, his choice was to bow to the Father's will and by so doing embrace the Father's will as his own. In other words, Jesus's prayer gives evidence of what we might call a holy ambivalence. I do not think that Jesus was merely acting out a role to make a point when he spoke these things. His prayer is a model, but it was also a genuine prayer. The agony was real, as was the expressed desire.

It is this reality that makes Jesus's prayer a model for us in our anger. When we admit our anger and frustration to God, we acknowledge our ambivalence. On the one hand, the fact that we are praying is itself a recognition of God's sovereignty. We pray because he is our God. We know that he is in control. In the act of praying, we begin with God and not our problem. By bringing our situation to him, we join the first disciples in addressing God as the sovereign Lord who made all things and in asking him to consider our situation (Acts 4:24–30).

At the same time, we often feel conflicted as well. Like Jonah, we are hunkered down and waiting to see what God will do for us. If we are not angry, we are at least frustrated by our circumstances. We wonder why

the sovereign God would allow such things to occur. This
note of frustration is frequently heard in the prayers of
the Bible. Abraham grumbles that since God has not
given him children, a servant must be his heir (Genesis
15:3). Moses complains because God has not granted
him the degree of success that he had expected. "Why,
Lord, why have you brought trouble on this people? Is
this why you sent me?" he says. "Ever since I went to
Pharaoh to speak in your name, he has brought trouble
on this people, and you have not rescued your people at
all" (Exodus 5:22–23). Hannah is so disappointed about
having no children that she cannot eat. She is so down-
hearted that she can hardly talk about it, and instead,
she pours out her anguish to God at Shiloh (1 Samuel
1:15–16).

These examples are hardly unusual. There are more
than twenty instances in the Psalms and the Prophets
where God's servants wonder, in a tone that we would
probably interpret as an indicator of impatience, how
long it will be before God answers their prayers. Indeed,
according to Revelation 6:10, even the saints in heaven
ask this question of God.

The surly tone and bluntness of these prayers shock
us. We are not sure that is appropriate to address God
this way. This is not how we sound when we pray. At
times our prayers are much more civil. So civil that they

are hardly more than spiritualized small talk. The problem, of course, is that if we decide to be as truthful as Jonah in our praying, we must also expose ourselves to the scrutiny of God's question: "Is it right for you to be angry?" We are pretty sure that we already know the answer.

Anger, Eugene Peterson has pointed out, is diagnostic. It tells us that something is wrong. "What anger fails to do, though, is tell us whether the wrong is outside us or inside us," he explains. "We usually begin by assuming that the wrong is outside us—our spouse or our child or our God has done something."[5] This is what Jonah does. He feels a burst of prophetic outrage and assumes that God is the problem. Jonah has a problem with God because he has a problem with the people of Nineveh. Jonah was angry about the evil of Nineveh. But mostly, he was angry because God did not seem to share his anger.

Jonah learned by experience what he already knew as a matter of intuition. When you pick a fight with God, you usually end up on the losing side. God is bigger than you are and has all the power. He holds all the cards and knows what you are going to say before you say it. Perhaps that was why Jonah's initial response was to flee. Maybe he thought it was better to run away than to stay and fight. What Jonah discovered is that it is impossible to run away from God. You cannot hide from him, not even when you pray. God does not deal gently with Jonah, but he does treat him kindly. By asking him the same question twice, God invited the prophet to examine his assumptions. This is the same question that he poses to us: "Is it right for you to be angry?"

Eugene Peterson points out that the Jonah story has no ending. "We are left with an unresolved scene: Jonah quarreling with God under the unpredictable plant and God delivering a heated reprimand punctuated with a question, 'And should not I pity Nineveh?' "[6]

We, too, are silent but often for a different reason. Sometimes ours is a silence born of fear. At other times it is the silence of artifice. Instead of expressing our real thoughts and feelings in prayer, we tell God what we think he wants to hear, as if God could not see through our charade, as if he did not already know what was in our hearts. It would be far better for us to take our stand with the patriarchs, the psalmists, and the prophets and state our feelings in plain words. It might be better, even, if we were to join Jonah as he sulks on the outskirts of Nineveh and risk engaging God in impolite conversation. Jonah, admittedly, is only barely obedient. But at least he is honest.

Chapter 5

Praying in the Words of Another

Pray like this three times a day.
—Didache 9:3

The first prayer that I remember praying was one I learned. It was a bedtime prayer. I don't recall whether I learned it from my mother or someone else. It went like this:

> Now I lay me down to sleep,
> I pray the Lord my soul to keep.
> If I should die before I wake,
> I pray the Lord my soul to take.

To be honest, this prayer disturbed me. Up to that point, it had not occurred to me that I could die in my sleep. The possibility terrified me. This sounded to me more like an invitation for God to take my life than a prayer for divine protection.

Many people who struggle with prayer have found it helpful to pray using the words of others. Sometimes these are rote prayers, like the bedtime prayer I learned to recite as a child. Others pray written prayers that are often published in a collection. The most famous sacred prayer is probably the Lord's Prayer, a prayer that has been prayed privately and collectively ever since the time of Christ. Most Christian traditions, both Catholic and Protestant, have published prayer books to help when prayer is difficult and to remind us of the promises and nature of God.

My Christian experience began among people who looked down on ritual and written prayers. They believed that the best prayers were spontaneous, framed in one's own words. Liturgical prayers (prayers that were memorized and repeated) were part of what they viewed as dead traditionalism, and written prayers were even worse. Although their thinking, as I hope to show shortly, was somewhat prejudiced on this matter, there is a legitimate danger in praying another's words instead of your own. If they are uttered without thought or meaning, such prayers can leave us "babbling like pagans," more interested in piling up sacred words than in expressing our heart (Matthew 6:7).

C. S. Lewis spoke of an "undeveloped type" of praying by those who repeat "whatever little formula they were taught in childhood by their mothers" and little else. "I wonder how this can come about," he marvels. "It can't be that they are never penitent or thankful—they're dear people, many of them—or have not needs."[1] Lewis seems to have felt that bland recitation was symptomatic of a disconnect between religion and real life. Yet, it is just as easy for so-called extemporaneous prayer to be undeveloped and unreflective. Often, extemporaneous prayer is not spontaneous at all but a repetition of phrases and themes that have been learned from listening to the prayers of others.

Learning to Pray by Imitation

This isn't necessarily a bad thing. Everyone learns to talk by listening to the conversations of others. The vocabulary of prayer is much the same. Indeed, there is plenty of evidence in the New Testament that the early church learned to pray primarily by imitation. One prominent example of this is the form of prayer that Jesus taught when his disciples asked him to teach them how to pray. According to Luke 11:1, Jesus introduced the prayer with the words: "When you pray, say …" Matthew's version begins with a similar command: "This is how you should pray …" (Matthew 6:9). The prayer's petitions, which are voiced using the first-person plural, also imply that Jesus expected the church to recite it together (Luke 11:3–4; Matthew 6:11–13).

Some Christians are uncomfortable praying the Lord's Prayer verbatim. They claim that it was not meant to be repeated word for word. Instead, Jesus's words are supposed to serve as an outline or general template. The specific petitions in the prayer give us an idea of the kinds of things we should be praying about. But Luke's version of the prayer includes an explicit command to repeat the words of the prayer as recited by Jesus. By the second century, however, the African theologian and apologist Tertullian urged Christians not only to pray the Lord's Prayer as prescribed, but to "build on it a structure of other petitions for occasional needs."[2]

Similarly, in his book *The Teacher*, Augustine, another African church leader who lived in the fourth and fifth centuries, records a dialogue with his sixteen-year-old son Adeodatus. Their conversation begins with the observation that prayer does not provide God with information that he does not already know. God's knowledge is so complete that we do not even have to speak out loud when we pray. God is sought "in the secret place of the rational soul," which the Bible calls "the inner man." When Adeodatus agreed with him, Augustine asked: "And you are not disturbed by the fact that our great Master, in teaching his disciples to pray, taught them what words to use in prayer?"

"No, that does not disturb me," Adeodatus replied. "For he did not teach them words merely, but by words, by means of which they could keep themselves in constant remembrance, he taught them realities—what they should pray for, and from whom, when they prayed in their inmost mind, as we said."[3]

From its earliest days, the church has prayed in both modes—sometimes by praying the words of others verbatim and sometimes using their prayers as a guide. It does not have to be an either/or choice. We can pray the Lord's Prayer word for word as Christ delivered it to the church, and we can use it as a template by adding concerns that are specific to our lives.

Ritual prayer was a standard feature of Jewish worship, and the prayers of the earliest Christians, like those of Jesus, were shaped by this tradition. Andrew B. McGowan explains, "Prayer for the first Christians involved far more than forming and expressing individual ideas and words; it was profoundly communal as well as highly personal, and a matter of body as well as mind."[4] One of the first pictures we have of the church is that of a church that prayed together. This is where we find the disciples immediately after Christ's ascension. They returned to Jerusalem and went upstairs to the room where they were staying: "They all joined together constantly in prayer, along with the women and Mary the mother of Jesus, and with his brothers" (Acts 1:14).

Two questions immediately come to mind. First, how could they pray *constantly*? Second, what did they *say*? Jesus commanded the disciples not to leave Jerusalem until they received the gift of the Holy Spirit that he had promised (Acts 1:4). The Spirit was poured out on Pentecost, seven weeks after Easter Sunday. When I pray, my mind wanders after only a few minutes! Did they really engage in a marathon prayer session that lasted seven weeks? Surely they had to take breaks for eating and sleeping. Indeed, we know that they stopped at least once to conduct business. Acts 1:15–26 says that "in those days," the disciples took time to choose someone to replace the traitor Judas.

New Testament scholar Joachim Jeremias sheds light on both questions when he points out that the early church followed the Jewish practice of praying three times daily. The book of Acts speaks of the apostles going up to the temple "at the time of prayer" (Acts 3:1). Likewise, both Peter and Cornelius observed the custom of afternoon prayer around three o'clock (Acts 10:3, 30). "The picture which emerges from our examination of the gospels is repeated when we turn to the *early church*," Jeremias explains. "Here too, as in contemporary Judaism and as in the life of Jesus, we find the three hours of prayer to be a firmly established practice."[5]

However, Jeremias notes that neither Jesus nor the church limited themselves to the customary three prescribed hours of prayer. Jesus spent extended time in prayer, often praying through the night or in the early morning hours. The church also prayed at the prescribed times and at other times as well. The church prayed through the night when Peter was imprisoned (Acts 12:5, 12). Paul also frequently used the language of continual prayer (Romans 1:9; Ephesians 6:18; Philippians 1:4; Colossians 1:3; 1 Thessalonians 5:17; 2 Thessalonians 1:3, 11; 2:13; 1 Timothy 5:5; 2 Timothy 1:3; Philemon 4). We could chalk this up to a hyperbole born out of enthusiasm, but Jeremias offers a more reasonable suggestion: "When he says that he prays 'continually', 'without ceasing', 'always', 'day and night', we are not to think of uninterrupted praying but of his observance of regular hours of prayer."[6]

The Church's Prayer Book

As for the content of these prayers, it seems likely that it was a mixture of praying based on tradition, quotes from the Psalms, and specific requests arising out of their circumstances. Jeremias suggests that the church's habit of daily praying involved a recitation of the Tefilla, a series of blessings that were sung. When the Tefilla was sung in the morning, it was recited along with the Shema, a confession of faith that combined phrases from Deuteronomy 6:4–9 and 11:13–21, and Numbers 15:37–41. In the evening, the Tefilla was recited alone. In addition, those who prayed added their own personal requests.[7] The Didache, a second-century manual of church practice, directed that the Lord's Prayer be prayed three times a day, perhaps replacing the Tefilla.

The Didache also prescribed a prayer for the cup when the church observed the Lord's Supper:

> We give you thanks, our Father,
> For the holy vine of David your servant,
> Which you have made known to us
> through Jesus, your servant;
> to you be the glory forever.[8]

After the cup, the congregation prayed this way for the bread:

> We give you thanks, our Father,
> for the life and knowledge
> that you have made known to us
> through Jesus, your servant;
> to you be the glory forever.
> Just as this broken bread was scattered
>   upon the mountains

and then was gathered together and
   became one,
so may your church be gathered together
   from the ends of
the earth into your kingdom;
for yours is the glory and the power
   through Jesus Christ forever.[9]

The Didache includes a prescribed prayer of thanksgiving to be prayed after everyone has "had enough":

We give you thanks, Holy Father,
For your holy name, which you have caused
   to dwell in our hearts,
And for the knowledge and faith and
   immortality that you
Have made known to us through Jesus your
   servant;
to you be the glory forever.
You, almighty Master, created all things for
   your name's sake,
and gave food and drink to humans to
   enjoy, so that they might give you thanks;
but to us you have graciously given spiritual food and drink,
and eternal life through your servant.
Above all we give thanks to you because
   you are mighty;

To you be the glory forever.
Remember your church, Lord,
to deliver it from all evil and to make it
    perfect in your love;
and from the four winds gather the church
    that has been
sanctified into your kingdom,
which you have prepared for it;
for yours is the power and the glory forever.
May grace come, and may this world pass
    away.
Hosanna to the God of David.
If anyone is holy, let him come;
If any one is not, let him repent.
Maranatha! Amen.[10]

These directions on how to pray during the Lord's Supper conclude with a curious exception: "But permit the prophets to give thanks however they wish."[11] Whatever the reason for this, it is clear that most worshipers prayed the words of these prayers verbatim. This does not mean that spontaneous prayers were generally frowned upon, only that some prayers followed a set form.

We know that the early Christians, like the Jews before them, often used the Psalms as a basis for prayer. Jonah prayed phrases of the Psalms while in the belly of the fish. Mary's prayer poem in Luke 1:46–55, known as the Magnificat, was infused with themes and language drawn from the Psalms and other portions of Scripture. As we saw in the previous chapter, Jesus prayed Psalm 22:1 from the cross. The church in Jerusalem quoted from Psalm 2 after the religious leaders commanded Peter and John to cease teaching or speaking in the name of Jesus (Acts 4:23–31).

This mixed pattern of recitation combined with personal request shows that the Psalms are more than a prayer book. They do not prescribe so much as they grant permission. The prayers of the Psalms free us from the restraints of self-consciousness and religious posturing. Their emotional honesty is proof that prayer is not merely a polite exchange between the worshiper and God. "The Psalms are an extended refutation that prayer is 'being nice' before God," Eugene Peterson observes. "No—prayer is an offering of ourselves, just as we are."[12] Their no-holds-barred emotional quality explains why the Psalms were not only the church's first prayer book but its first songbook.

Given its roots in Judaism, it is no surprise that singing from the Psalms had an important place in the church's prayer life. After the Last Supper, Jesus sang Psalms with his disciples before going out to the Mount of Olives (Matthew 26:30; Mark 14:26). The Passover tradition concluded with a prayer of thanksgiving and

Psalms 114–118 sung antiphonally. One person sang the half-verse, and the others at the table responded with "Hallelujah." Joachim Jeremias conjectures that because Jesus was the one with the greatest knowledge of Scripture, he probably sang the verses while the other disciples gave the responses. "However that may be, whether he recited it or only joined in the prayers and responses, we know the prayers with which Jesus concluded the Last Supper," Jeremias observes. "They are all prayers of thanksgiving."[13]

When we look to the Psalms as a template for our own prayers, we quickly discover that we have much to say. "As we do this, the first thing we realize is that in prayer anything goes," Eugene Peterson explains. "Virtually everything human is appropriate as material for prayer: reflections and observations, fear and anger, guilt and sin, questions and doubts, needs and desires, praise and gratitude, suffering and death. Nothing human is excluded."[14]

We are not saying these things for God's benefit but our own. Many people find it helpful to share such things with a therapist, who can do nothing about these feelings. How much more should we share them with a God who can? Scripture tells us to do so. James 5:13 declares, "Is anyone among you in trouble? Let them pray. Is anyone happy? Let them sing songs of praise."

The Greek word that the NIV translates "trouble" into is a general term that refers to misfortunes of all sorts. New Testament scholar Peter Davids points out that "the inner experience of having to endure misfortune is indicated more than a specific form of misfortune" in this verse.[15] But troubles are not the only reason we pray. James also urges those who are happy to pray. One does not necessarily have to be in better circumstances to do this. Douglas Moo points out that the Greek word translated as "happy" refers "not to outward circumstances, but to the cheerfulness and happiness of heart that one can have whether in good times or in bad."[16]

Singing Our Prayers

The specific mode of prayer that James recommends for the cheerful is song. The word that is translated "sing songs of praise" is a Greek term that literally meant "to play on a harp." It is related to the word for a psalm and is a reminder of the value of using the book of Psalms as a resource for our own prayers as well as the vital role that singing plays in our overall prayer life. We are used to thinking of singing as an act of worship. Indeed, for many in the church, singing is worship. But singing is also prayer. If we need more proof beyond the command of James 5:13 that song is an appropriate vehicle for prayer, we need not look any further than Jesus Christ.

"When praying to his Father in heaven, Jesus, the Word incarnate, did not shun the use of human words, human gestures, and human postures; likewise, he did not shun human music," Michael O'Connor points out.[17]

Calling Christ "the leader and initiator of Christian worship" and its "High Priest of the sacrifice of praise," based on Hebrews 8:1–2, O'Connor suggests further that Christ, who taught his disciples to pray and sang with them, continues to sing with the church. "Christ sings among his people when they are gathered to worship on earth," he explains. "This is part of his promise to remain among them even to the ends of the age (Matt. 28:20)."[18] If true, O'Connor's intriguing proposal radically changes our perception of what is going on when we sing. We tend to think of Christ as the passive recipient of our worship. We sing, and he listens. If O'Connor is correct, our voices are transformed into a kind of participation in Christ's ministry of intercessory prayer. As we pray through song, Christ prays as well, presenting our praise and petition to the Father on our behalf. Even if what O'Connor suggests is pure speculation, clearly the early church recognized singing as a legitimate mode of prayer.

Another revealing feature of the command of James 5:13 is the connection that it makes between music and emotion. We know from experience that music has an affective quality. Most of us do not choose our music based on its technical quality but because of the way it makes us feel. The same is true of the church. Today's church tends to use music to create a mood and to attract visitors. Worship and music are so identified that if someone says that we are going to worship, most people will assume they mean we are going to sing. According to Andrew McGowan, "This would have baffled Christians of the first centuries," for whom "music was neither the most central or distinctive aspect of their gatherings nor identified with 'worship' as such, any more than other activities were."[19]

Ironically, when Acts 2:42 describes the priorities of the first disciples, it does not mention music or even worship. Instead, it says that they "devoted themselves to the apostles' teaching and to fellowship, to the breaking of bread and to prayer." Yet, the New Testament does show that music had an important place in the early church. Paul and Silas sang through the night while in prison (Acts 16:25). John's vision of heaven's worship includes singing with musical instruments (Revelation 5:9; 14:2–3). John does not describe the melody, only its overall effect. He says that it was "like the roar of rushing waters and like a loud peal of thunder" (Revelation 14:2).

James 5:13 illustrates another major difference in thinking. Instead of prescribing music in the hope that it will make us feel a certain way, James recommends singing as a vehicle of expression. He does not tell us to sing in order to feel but urges us to sing because we feel. This underscores the unique place of music as a form of prayer. When we pray, we are trying to express things that go beyond words.

Singing enables us to express ourselves in words just as we would with ordinary prayer, but it is also an expression that goes beyond speech. When we sing, we express our emotions as well as our thoughts. Furthermore, there is a physical dimension to music-making. Its sonic nature resonates with us on our deepest level in the most literal sense. "Music is a very bodily business, whether or not the human voice is used," Jeremy Begbie explains. "Our physical, physiological, and neurological makeup shapes the making and hearing of music to a high degree."[20] Singing enables us to pray with the whole person and not only with words.

Music also has a reciprocal dimension. It enables us to express our feelings to God even as it arouses emotion within us. This makes singing uniquely suited to the kind of twofold expression that Paul describes in Ephesians 5:19 and Colossians 3:16, where he directs the church to speak to God and to each other simultaneously using psalms, hymns, and spiritual songs.

Music's ability to arouse emotion was one reason the Reformation theologian and pastor John Calvin cautioned, "We should be very careful that our ears be not more attentive to the melody than our minds to the spiritual meaning of the words."[21] Calvin's warning underscores two difficulties we often face where church music is concerned. Calvin's primary concern was the danger that we will be more interested in the music than the message. We may be so caught up in the music that we pay little attention to the words. When we respond in this way, we do not really speak to God, nor does the message of the music speak to us. We are caught up in the emotion of the moment—feeling but not thinking.

The error in this sort of worship is essentially the same one that the Corinthian church fell into when it practiced the gift of tongues without interpretation. It leaves the mind behind. Paul makes it clear that the mind matters in our worship and our prayer: "So what shall I do? I will pray with my spirit, but I will also pray with my understanding; I will sing with my spirit, but I will also sing with my understanding" (1 Corinthians 14:15).

Calvin wasn't merely urging the congregation to pay attention when they sang. He was especially concerned that they would sing the truth. We are being formed by the words that we vocalize, but we are not always asking how closely those words conform to the truth of God's word. As a form of instruction and mode of prayer, the church's singing has a major role in shaping how we should both think about God and approach him.

The other difficulty Calvin's warning highlights has to do with style and preference. We do not all enjoy the same music. The often-voiced complaint that someone "just can't worship to that kind of music" is not without merit. Our musical tastes are shaped by experience.

The power of context is nicely illustrated in Thomas Troeger's description of the times he sat with his mother at the piano as a child as she played hymns that he never heard in church. "Opening a tattered old hymnal to play her favorites, she would often remark, 'They don't sing the hymns I know, and they don't sing with the warmth we used to sing in our little church home,'" he writes.[22] Troeger could sense a difference. "As a child I recognized immediately the difference in the sound, and with a child's way of knowing, I sensed two different musical characterizations of God in the contrasting tunes and rhythms," he explains. "The words of 'In the G'rden' always made me picture my great-aunt's flower garden where I used to weed with her 'n the early morning when I visited my mother's childhood home. And the words of 'O God of Bethel by Whose Hand' always brought to mind a picture in my history textbook of the Pilgrims in New England simply because the first verse speaks of 'this weary pilgrimage.'"[23]

In Psalm 137, the writer tells how the Israelite exiles in Babylon sat and wept when they remembered their former home. "There on the poplars we hung our harps, for there our captors asked us for songs, our tormentors demanded songs of joy; they said, 'Sing us one of the songs of Zion!'" the psalmist laments. "How can we sing the songs of the LORD while in a foreign land?" (Psalm 137:1–4). Sometimes we find it hard to sing the prayers they ask us to in church because they are not the tunes we know or like. At other times we have trouble singing because of the song's discordant tone. The Babylonian exiles could not sing because their captors demanded songs of joy when their hearts were broken. The same is often true of the church, especially when it employs music as a tool to create atmosphere or attract visitors. In either case, the musical language that we are asked to use is someone else's. It does not feel like our voice or our heart. Worship leaders who sense the disconnect may badger worshipers to join in even when their hearts are not in it by reminding the congregation that worship "is not about us." Perhaps they are right. But if singing is prayer, then if it is not about us, it still involves our hearts.

At such times, the best thing to do may be to "hang up your harp" and carry on a counter dialogue with God in the old-fashioned way. If you cannot sing, then pray in silence. Speak to God from your heart and in your own voice. You are not performing for God. You do not have to work yourself into an emotional state that matches the music that the worship leader has chosen. If the essence of worship is to offer yourself to God, then the place to begin is to offer your true self. If you are grieving, then offer him your grieving self. If you are angry, then offer him your angry self. If you are worried, then offer him your worried self. As James so wisely put it: "Is anyone among you in trouble? Let them pray. Is anyone happy? Let them sing songs of praise."

Learning to Speak in Another Voice

The main thing that troubles those who are uncomfortable with memorized prayer is its liturgical nature. It bothers them that the words they pray are not their own words. Until they pray them so often that they become second nature, it feels as if they are speaking to God in someone else's voice. But is this really such a bad thing? The fact that some forms of prayer are ritualized speech is not necessarily a condemning factor either. Dead rituals can indeed pose a danger, but in such cases, it is the deadness, not the fact that they are rituals, that poses the problem. Rituals are merely repeated actions that become meaningful to us by their repetition. James K. A. Smith has defined rituals as "material, embodied routines that we do over and over again; they are usually aimed at a specific end, or goal; and their repetition and practice has the effect of making them more and more automatic such that they become part of the very fiber of our character, wired into our second nature."[24]

These kinds of traditions can be great or small. Great traditions are practiced by many people and are not local to a specific group or region. Practices like the Lord's Supper and baptism fall into this category. Small traditions are specific to groups, regions, and even individuals. The fact that your church has a meal after the Sunday service each week is a small tradition. It is meaningful to your church, but not every church does it. The fact that we pray is a great tradition. All of God's people do this. Prayers like the Lord's Prayer also fit here. Some Christian traditions prescribe certain prayers for public and private worship. But if you listen to the way people pray when the church comes together, you will soon discover that even non-traditional churches employ patterns of repetition when they pray. They may address God as "Our heavenly Father" and close with the phrase "in Jesus's name." Sometimes they include traits that are learned and repeated but not especially meaningful in themselves. We pray at the same times and ask for the same things, often employing the same phrases.

Some kind of rote praying is a feature of every Christian tradition, just as every church has its own liturgy, whether it is formal or informal. "All Christian worship—whether Anglican or Anabaptist, Pentecostal or Presbyterian—is liturgical in the sense that it is governed by norms, draws on a tradition, includes bodily rituals or routines, and involves formative practices," James K. A. Smith observes.[25]

Everybody who learns to pray begins by praying words they have heard from others. In a way, none of us begins by praying in our own voice. We must first learn a vocabulary and a pattern of speech. It shows us what to ask for and how to ask. It enables us to put into words feelings and desires for which we previously had no name. Over time, what once sounded like an unfamiliar voice eventually becomes a way to find our own.

Chapter 6

How to Stay Focused During Prayer

Watch and pray so that you will not fall into temptation.
The spirit is willing, but the flesh is weak.
—*Matthew 26:41*

Many things can get in the way of praying. But for me, the most common obstacle may be boredom. I sometimes find prayer tedious. I suppose I shouldn't admit such a thing, but there it is. I find it hard to stay focused. My prayers all sound the same to me. They begin and end the same way. They seem to be composed of the same requests uttered day after day in the same words. Listening to myself pray can be about as interesting as reading a form letter. Not that prayer has to be interesting to be effective. Prayer is an interchange, not a performance.

Nor, perhaps, should I even be troubled by the fact that I can get bored when I pray. Various factors influence the way we feel, none of which necessarily have any bearing on the actual outcome. We may be tired or sick. We may be afraid. The fact that I state my request unimaginatively means nothing to God, who does not analyze our style but searches the heart (Romans 8:27). Yet, it occurs to me that the monotony of prayer could be of my own making. The vocabulary that the Bible uses to speak of prayer is more expansive than my practice. Perhaps I am bored because I am only praying one kind of prayer when in reality, there are many.

All Kinds of Prayers

One intimation of how much variety there is in prayer is reflected in Paul's command in Ephesians 6:18, which urges believers to "pray in the Spirit on all occasions with all kinds of prayers and requests." In this verse, the apostle refers to two broad categories of variation. One involves circumstances. He urges believers to pray "on all occasions." One of the things that makes prayer interesting, for lack of a better word, is the situation that prompts it. Just as we explored in the last chapter that there are great and small traditions, we might also say that there are great and small prayers. It is unreasonable to expect every prayer to be a transcendent experience.

Sometimes our prayers are urgent. We turn to God in a moment of great need. In those moments, we reach for God the way a drowning swimmer reaches for the outstretched arm of a lifeguard. We have skin in the game. Those are often the times when we feel God's presence the most. We can say with the conviction of the psalmist, "In my distress I called to the LORD; I cried to my God for help. From his temple he heard my voice; my cry came before him, into his ears" (Psalm 18:6).

At other times, the circumstances that prompt our prayers are mundane. We say grace before a meal or at the beginning of some task we are about to undertake. We run through the names on our prayer list and generally ask for God's blessing on their lives. We are not too specific because we are not aware of any remarkable need. The more ordinary the context, the less emotionally charged the experience. The point of prayer is not to have an emotional experience. Most of our lives are made up of ordinary days. Just as an athlete's regular training outside the game produces the muscle memory that will enable them to perform in the heat of competition, the habit of ordinary prayer trains us to respond prayerfully in the moment of crisis. Ordinary prayer sanctifies the mundane and makes the benign beautiful.

There is nothing wrong with beginning or ending something with prayer. The Bible is full of these sorts of prayers. It is inattention that creates the problem. When our prayers become so common that all we are doing is making religious noise, they cease to be prayers.

Invocations and benedictions are prayers located at the opposite ends of a task or an endeavor. When a church service begins, sometimes the pastor or worship leader will offer an invocation. This is a kind of invitation offered to God, although we shouldn't think that he needs permission from us to be part of the service, nor should we think that he is somewhere outside the building waiting to be let in. In a way, an invocation is a reminder to ourselves that God is already present as much as it is an invitation to God.

A benediction is a blessing. It asks God to bless what we have done or to continue to help us. Although benedictions are viewed as prayers, often they are not addressed to God at all but to the congregation. They are a promise addressed to God's people. When my children were small, my wife Jane and I would pray the priestly blessing from Numbers 6:24–26 over them when they went to bed:

> The LORD bless you
>   and keep you;
> the LORD make his face shine on you
>   and be gracious to you;
> the LORD turn his face toward you
>   and give you peace.

Jane would always add the phrase "and a good night's sleep" at the end. When I was a pastor, I often prayed the same blessing over the congregation at the end of the worship service (without the request for a good night's sleep).

The Bible employs several words when speaking of prayer. The most basic term is "ask." It is the general word that Paul uses in Philippians 4:6: "Do not be anxious about anything, but in every situation, by prayer and petition, with thanksgiving, present your *requests* to God." A prayer is simply an ask. But Paul's inclusion of two additional terms expands the definition. Paul calls these requests "prayers" and "petitions." These same terms are in Ephesians 6:18. If there is a difference between them, it is a difference in perspective. The term prayer looks at it from God's direction. It was the word commonly used to refer to a request addressed to a deity. This language reminds us of the relational dynamic that provides the context for our request. We are coming to God, who is greater than we are. In a sense, it is a word that puts us in our place.

The first two verses from John Newton's hymn entitled "Come, My Soul, With Every Care" shows the face we pray to:

> Come, my soul, with ev'ry care;
> Jesus loves to answer prayer.
> He himself bids you to pray.
> He will never turn away,
> he will never turn away.

You are coming to a king—
large petitions with you bring.
For his grace and pow'r are such,
none can ever ask too much,
none can ever ask too much.

Keep Calm and Pray On

A petition, on the other hand, looks at prayer from our
angle. A petition expresses what we want. The Greek
word speaks of beseeching or begging someone. It is
more than a request; this is an earnest request. Newton's
hymn speaks of this as well. It urges that we bring "large
petitions" and assures us that no legitimate request is
"too much" for God.

So, the first principle to help us stay interested is to
have clarity about what we are doing and what we want.
What exactly do we want? What are we asking? It is
shockingly easy to pray absentmindedly. Our petitions
are not petitions at all. They are not specific enough. We
ask God to bless us but in a very general sense. So general, in fact, that God could not answer them if he were
limited only to the specifics we share. Fortunately, he is
able to see past our vague requests to the real needs that
lie beneath them. But it is hard for us to stay attentive
without a concrete sense of what we need. It is not selfish to think about yourself and your situation before
you pray.

The danger is that we will get so caught up with our problems that we will lose sight of God. These two things, an awareness of God and our need, should both be kept in view. But that does not mean that we give them equal weight or even equal attention. Like a prayer meeting where people spend all their time reviewing their troubles in detail but only a few minutes talking to God about them, we can become lost in the fog of our concerns when we pray. That's why Paul adds a note about expectation in Philippians 4:6. He says that we should bring our petitions "with thanksgiving." He might just as easily have said faith. Faith is clearly behind this statement. However, by expressing it as thanksgiving, Paul invites us to position ourselves as those who have already seen their prayers answered. This is not visualization, positive thinking, or claiming the specific answer you want. This faith focuses on God more than on the nature of the problem or the specifics of his answer. It assumes that God will answer without prescribing how he should respond. The details are left to him.

It only makes sense that we should have our problems in mind when we pray. They are the concerns that motivate us to go to God in the first place. But it is possible that in the process, we may magnify those concerns so much that they drive God from our minds. Sometimes when we pray, we are only worrying out loud to God.

God hears even these prayers, but they don't bring us much comfort.

You have probably seen a version of the bright red poster with a crown that says KEEP CALM AND CARRY ON somewhere on the web. There is an infinite number of variations of this saying plastered on T-shirts, coffee cups, and bumper stickers. The first poster was produced in 1939 by the British government to boost morale as World War II loomed on the horizon. Long before this, 1 Peter 4:7 offered similar advice in connection with prayer: "The end of all things is near. Therefore be alert and of sober mind so that you may pray." Peter's version of this saying might be: KEEP CALM AND PRAY ON.

Fear can be an impetus to pray, but panic can be a great hindrance. When it takes hold of our thinking, it exhausts our energy, deriving its momentum from a combination of fear and speculation. We do not look at God, but at our problems, and the more we focus on our problems, the specter of what they might become blossoms in our minds. Our problems are real, but fear and speculation magnify them, causing us to run ahead in our thinking to all the things that might happen to us because of them. There is no way to defend ourselves against these speculations because they are what-ifs. We can take no steps to address them. Even the plans we make in our minds do us little good because as soon as we devise a strategy for one possibility, another arises in our minds.

Peter's remedy begins with the mind. Peter says that we must take steps to get our thinking under control by being clear-minded and controlled in our judgment. We might characterize this as realistic thinking in tandem with biblical realism, enabling us to keep God in view along with our problems. Biblical realism does not downplay problems, nor does it allow the imagination to get carried away. Sometimes the best question to ask yourself is, "What is the worst that can happen?" The worst that can happen is often not as bad as the things we fantasize might happen to us.

We often do not have control over our circumstances. Nor do we always have control over our feelings. They usually begin as an involuntary response. But we can control the way we think about both our circumstances and feelings. When Peter urges believers to be alert, he employs the word that described the Gerasene demoniac's condition after the legion of demons left him. The people of the town found him "in his right mind" (Mark 5:15). The word that describes the kind of thinking Peter calls for is "prudent." Prudence is not an outdated Victorian virtue. It is a word that Scripture uses to express the notion of discipline and restraint. Peter uses it in conjunction with the word "sober," which originally described a condition that was the opposite of intoxication. In the New Testament, however, it is figurative and speaks of self-control.

The picture Peter offers is not just of someone who prays but of someone who thinks. More than this, it is a picture of someone who thinks about the way they are thinking. They are not passive and reactive, allowing their minds to be overwhelmed by circumstances and their thoughts to run away with themselves. The situation we find ourselves in may provide the impetus for prayer, but the content of that prayer should grow out of reflection.

Peter provides a theological framework for this realism by placing it within an eschatological context. He says that the "end of all things" is at hand. At first glance, this hardly seems helpful. The cry "the end of the world is coming," sounds more like a recipe for panic than its cure. But instead of viewing the approaching end as a cataclysm, Peter saw it as a completion. It is a point of view shaped by the second and third petitions of the Lord's Prayer: "Your kingdom come, your will be done, on earth as it is in heaven" (Matthew 6:10).

For the Christian, the troubles that call for prayer are bound up with all the other things that God is doing. This is a perspective shaped by faith that includes not only a sense of history but of destiny. Our lives, even in the worst situation, are not running out of control. They are tending toward an end that God has designed. This world's disorder, precipitated by sin's entrance, will eventually give way to a new order when Christ comes with his kingdom. Instead of making prayer unnecessary, this inevitability calls for it. Peter does not tell us that since the end that God has designed is at hand, we can ignore all the troubles we face. Nor does he seem to think that the progress of God's plan is detached from our activity. We do not bring in the kingdom by our efforts, but neither are we easing into it. We are more than passive agents who sit idly by and wait. We are active and engaged. Instead, the apostle tells us to keep our thinking under control so that we can pray.

Praying is a spiritual act, but it is also a cognitive act that requires focused attention. Everyone knows the frustration of having a conversation with someone who is distracted. Perhaps it is because their mind wanders, flitting from one topic to another. Or it may be a result of multi-tasking—the one with whom we are trying to converse is doing something else at the same time. Their attention is divided. Prayer is no different. Conversation with God, just like a conversation with any other person, requires that we concentrate on the topic at hand and on the one to whom we wish to speak. "In this matter, the harder we find concentration to be, the more strenuously we ought to labor after it," John Calvin observes with his usual common sense. "For no one is so intent on praying that he does not feel many irrelevant thoughts stealing upon him, which either break the course of prayer or delay it by some winding bypath."[1]

A meaningful prayer experience requires some forethought. First, what is the subject that we have come to God to talk about? Second, what exactly do we want to say? If we had an appointment with our employer that we knew would cover important topics related to our job, we would spend some time thinking in advance about what we planned to say. The same is true when we have a serious talk with a friend or a family member. We choose our words carefully so that we can express ourselves in just the right way. We do this, in part, so that they will not misunderstand us. But only in part. We choose our words carefully because we have something we want to express. This is what makes the conversation important to us. Although there is no danger that God will misunderstand us, there is a possibility that we may come to him without having much to say. Perhaps the reason we have trouble focusing during prayer is that the conversation *isn't* important. Our thoughts are muddled because we haven't given much thought to what we are trying to say.

Holy Kinesics and Sacred Spaces

Although words are primary, especially where prayer is concerned, we do not communicate with words alone. Gestures and body motions are also a kind of language. The technical word for this is kinesics. "Persons who cannot stand still, who rock back and forth, twiddle their thumbs, or tap their fingers are indicating impatience or nervousness," professor of international communication Donald K. Smith explains. "The person who is tired and bored sits in a chair differently from the person who is really interested in what is happening."[2] A wink, a nod, a slight gesture of the hand all indicate something. Kinesic signals can provide context for our words, or they may contradict them. We are less conscious of the kinesic signals we use in communication than the words we say.

Just as we do in ordinary communication, those who pray sometimes express themselves using kinesic signals. Posture, gestures, and various actions are part of the non-verbal vocabulary we use to talk to God. The difference between these holy kinesics and ordinary body language is that God does not need such signals to understand us. They are for our benefit. Moses's encounter with God in the burning bush is a prime example. As Moses tended Jethro's flock on the far side of the desert, he noticed a bush that was on fire but did not burn up. As he approached the bush, the Lord called out to him. "Do not come any closer," God said. "Take off your sandals, for the place where you are standing is holy ground" (Exodus 3:5).

The act of removing his sandals was a symbolic gesture, not done for God's benefit but for Moses's. It is a statement about Moses's relationship to God, but its message was aimed at Moses himself. The removal of his sandals was a forcible reminder to Moses that he was about to encounter God. Taking off his sandals did not make Moses holier than before, but it was a way to recognize this encounter's sacred nature. This action also marked the place where Moses stood as a sacred space, although this sacred quality was only temporary. Presumably, before God appeared to Moses, this was just another bush in the wilderness. After the encounter, the bush, and the ground upon which it stood, were returned to their former status. As far as we know, Moses did not rope off the area or return to it. This was just the first of many sacred moments and symbolic actions that would eventually be made formal in Israel's worship through the law.

The traditional posture of prayer is kneeling. The Old Testament prophet Daniel prayed on his knees three times daily (Daniel 6:10). Paul also mentions kneeling in Ephesians 3:14, saying that he "bends his knee" to the Father. To bow the knee to someone was an acknowledgment of their superiority. When Pharaoh made Joseph his second-in-command, the people were required to kneel as his chariot rode by (Genesis 41:43). When the apostle speaks of bowing the knee, it is a figure of speech as much as it is a literal description of what he does. To bow the knee is a metonymy, where the phrase stands in place of the word prayer.

Other postures are also mentioned in Scripture. In Mark 11:25 Jesus warns, "And when you stand praying, if you hold anything against anyone, forgive them, so that your Father in heaven may forgive you your sins." The reference to standing suggests that the location of this praying was in the temple. When Jesus prayed in distress in the Garden of Gethsemane, he "fell with his face to the ground" (Matthew 26:39). David even communed with God while lying in his bed at night (Psalm 63:6).

The most common gesture associated with prayer in Scripture is that of lifting one's hands (Psalm 141:2). Paul spoke of lifted hands as a symbolic act: "Therefore I want the men everywhere to pray, lifting up holy hands without anger or disputing" (1 Timothy 2:8). His real emphasis in this verse is on the moral character of those who pray. He wanted believers' hands to be holy and their relationship with one another to be characterized by peace.

In the second and third centuries, a variety of traditions were practiced as a matter of custom. Following the Jewish pattern, set hours for prayer were observed (nine o'clock, noon, and three o'clock) based on a rationale that often appealed to the Trinity. Those who prayed either stood or knelt, depending on the nature of the prayer. Standing was appropriate for praise, while kneeling was a sign of repentance. During this period, the stance known as *orans*, standing with eyes raised and hands outstretched with elbows close to the sides of the body, was commonly used in prayer. According to Andrew McGowan, "This cruciform praying body was then further marked with the cross as an additional act of physical prayer, in the gesture that has become known as the sign of the cross."[3]

Jesus signaled a radical shift when he told the Samaritan woman that a time was coming "when you will worship the Father neither on this mountain nor in Jerusalem" (John 4:21). This change meant that Jerusalem would no longer be the most important sacred space for God's people. While Jews often faced Jerusalem when they prayed, many Christians worshiped while facing east because Christ ascended toward the east and was expected to return "in the same way" (Acts 1:11; see also Matthew 24:27).[4] The believer's body is a temple of the Holy Spirit (1 Corinthians

6:19). In Christ, all believers "are being built together to become a dwelling in which God lives by his Spirit" (Ephesians 2:22). For Christians, every space can be a sacred space because their presence sanctifies it. Even the most painful circumstances have the potential to be a kind of sanctuary because God is present and the Holy Spirit is in them.

Things like posture and gestures can sometimes help us focus our attention when we pray. They may enable us to express ourselves more fully, not because God needs more clarity but because we do. They can also serve as reminders both of our purpose in prayer and the promises that shape it. Paying attention to the environment in which we pray can also be beneficial. In a study of the role of imagination and the arts in American spirituality, sociologist Robert Wuthnow observed that those who think Americans only pray by talking to God or reciting prayers from the Bible are mistaken. "It has become commonplace for people to listen to music while they pray, to seek the help of a favorite musician or writer to get them in the mood for prayer, to look at icons or hold mental pictures of Jesus in their minds when they pray, and to turn to music and art for comfort when they feel especially in need," he explains.[5] Wuthnow characterizes such things as ambiance and observes that most research on prayer has overlooked its importance: "Focusing instead on the idea that prayer is simply talking to God, researchers have examined the verbal content of prayer."[6]

Yet the church's history has also shown that aids like these can become a stumbling block. Instead of helping us they may become a distraction. At their worst, they lead to idolatry. Anthony Bloom, an archbishop in the Russian Orthodox Church explains the threat they pose in his book *Beginning to Pray.* "The moment you try to focus on an imaginary god, or a god you can imagine, you are in great danger of placing an idol between yourself and the real God," he writes. Bloom points out that the fourth-century theologian Gregory of Nazianzus warned of this very thing: "He said that the moment we put a visible sign in front of ourselves, whether it be a crucifix, a tabernacle, an icon or an invisible image— God as we imagine Him, or Christ as we have seen Him in paintings—and we focus our attention on that, then we have placed a barrier between ourselves and God, because we take the image which we have formed for the person to whom we address our prayer."[7]

It can also help our concentration to have a space that is sacred, in the sense that it has been set apart for the practice of prayer. It does not have to be large, fancy, or even overtly religious. A quiet room with a comfortable chair where you can spend time undistracted will be fine. Yet none of these things can substitute for spirit and truth. Nor can they make us more attentive to God on their own. If there is any benefit in adopting a particular posture or making a gesture, it is because it is meaningful to the one who prays. The sign is not sacred in itself. Such actions do not add value to the prayer in God's eyes. He does not give more weight to our requests because we make the sign of the cross or lie prostrate on the ground. Just as we should not think that we will be heard for our many words, we should not think that we will be heard for our many gestures (Matthew 6:7). Such things are helpful only to the one who prays.

The danger with all helps of this nature is that they often become substitutes for the task they were meant to aid. Instead of focusing our attention for the purpose of prayer they distract us from praying, either because we confuse the ritual with prayer or let it stand in place of our own thoughts or our own effort. We can become so fixated on the symbolic action that we begin to believe that our prayer's efficacy depends upon it. If we do not use this specific gesture or pray in this particular place, we have not prayed at all. Scripture makes it very clear that gestures can be empty. The prophets of Baal made a great show of dancing around the altar they had made and slashing themselves. The soldiers who mocked

Christ knelt before him in feigned reverence. Ananias and Sapphira laid their money at the apostles' feet with a flourish in a gesture of false devotion.

Reasonable Expectations

Not every conversation has the same gravity. At the Bible college where I taught, there was a small table in the corner of the student dining room that students referred to as the DTR table. The initials stood for "Defining the Relationship." The story was that couples sat there when they wanted to have a watershed conversation about their relationship. Were they dating or just friends? How serious were they?

It's doubtful that every couple who sat at the table had the DTR conversation, especially after it became known as the DTR table. Many who sat there were only having lunch and making small talk. A conversation does not have to be life-changing to be meaningful. The same is true with prayer. Every prayer does not have to be a defining moment to be worth praying. Some are only small prayers about the small things that occupy us. Is it possible that we come to prayer with unreasonable expectations about what the experience should be like? We have confused emotion with spirituality. The test of a prayer's legitimacy is not whether my heart feels strangely warmed after I prayed it or not. It is enough to ask and to know that God has heard me.

Maybe the real problem with my praying is that what I have been calling tedium is actually familiarity. I have come looking for a burning bush only to find a quiet room and a comfortable chair. God does not have to announce his arrival with a flourish. He is always with me because he dwells in me (John 14:17). Our momentary conversation does not have to be dramatic. It is enough to say my piece and then go my way.

Chapter 7

Jesus on Prayer

———

Lord, teach us to pray, just as John taught his disciples.
—Luke 11:1

Most people learn to pray by imitation. They hear the prayers of others and copy them. Jesus's disciples were different only in one regard. They learned how to pray from Jesus. This model prayer, usually referred to as the Lord's Prayer, is a prayer that we can pray for ourselves, but it is also a kind of template. By analyzing the categories Jesus mentions, we understand the types of requests we can make when we pray in our own words.

A Prayer We Can Pray

At its most basic level, the Lord's Prayer provides us with a foundational vocabulary for praying. The church received these words from Christ and for more than two millennia has prayed them back to God:

Our Father in heaven,

hallowed be your name,

your kingdom come,

your will be done,

on earth as it is in heaven.

Give us today our daily bread.

And forgive us our debts,

as we also have forgiven our debtors.

And lead us not into temptation,

but deliver us from the evil one,

for yours is the kingdom and the power

and the glory forever. Amen.

(Matthew 6:9–13)[1]

"The words of the Lord's Prayer are immediate to every situation in life," theologian Helmut Thielicke observes.[2] It is a prayer that can be prayed privately or with others. When we don't know what to say, it is a comfort to know that we can pray these words at all times and in every situation. According to Andrew McGowan, "The first readers of the Gospels did not think of the Lord's Prayer primarily as a model or primer about prayer, although it may have been that too; for them, the first point was actually to *say* it."[3] It is no surprise, then, that the Lord's Prayer appears in the early manual of church practice known as the Didache, whose origin may go back as far as the early part of the second century. It says to "pray like this three times a day."[4] In the fourth century, congregations recited the Lord's Prayer together as part of public worship connected with the Lord's Supper.

However, for the early church, the Lord's Prayer was not the people's prayer that it is today. For us, the Lord's Prayer is the common property of religious and irreligious people alike. Most people know it (or at least bits and pieces of it). Ambrose, the fourth-century bishop of Milan who was a mentor to St. Augustine, felt that the Lord's Prayer should only be taught to those who were true initiates in the Christian faith.[5] This may seem harsh to us today. But it is consistent with Christ's own prayer for his church on the night of his betrayal and arrest: "I pray for them. I am not praying for the world, but for those you have given me, for they are yours" (John 17:9).

Just as Christ's prayer was for us, these words of the Lord's Prayer handed down to us by Christ are also ours. They are proof of God's care for us and of the new relationship that has come to us through Jesus Christ. The first proof of this is in the manner of address that Jesus teaches us to use when reciting the Lord's Prayer. We begin by calling God "our Father." The idea of God as father was not unknown before this. Psalm 103:13–14 says, "As a father has compassion on his children, so the LORD has compassion on those who fear him; for he knows how we are formed, he remembers that we are dust." Israel was called God's firstborn son (Exodus 4:22; Jeremiah 31:9). In the New Testament, Paul speaks of "adoption as sons" as one of Israel's advantages (Romans 9:3).[6] But this adoption is framed primarily as a national rather than a personal experience. Although the fatherhood of God is implicit in the Old Testament, people were more likely to view themselves as God's servants than his children. They addressed him as Lord more than Father.

Before giving his disciples the words to this prayer, Jesus prepared them to receive it by warning of two major dangers related to prayer. One is the temptation to pray without really speaking to God. Those who do so pray "to be seen by others" (Matthew 6:5). This is probably a reference to the Jewish practice of observing set times for prayer. Like Muslims today, Jews had specific times set aside when they stopped to pray. The scenario that Jesus paints is one where a person seems to go out of their way to be as visible as possible when the time arrived. Their fault was not that they stood up to pray in the synagogue or prayed on the street corner. It was the fact that they "loved to stand up" in these places "to be seen." When our praying becomes a performance, it ceases to be prayer. God disappears from view, as does the request that we make. Jesus's counsel, in such cases, is to take measures to remove yourself from the spotlight. "But when you pray, go into your room, close the door and pray to your Father, who is unseen. Then your Father, who sees what is done in secret, will reward you" (Matthew 6:6).

When I was a new believer, I took Jesus's words literally and tried to pray in my bedroom closet. It didn't last long. It might have worked better for me if I had cleaned my closet first. Jesus's statement is figurative, a kind of hyperbole that means we should make every effort to be sure that our praying is intended for God. Step off the stage. Get out of the street. Keep your seat in the assembly and save your praying for when you get home. Jesus does not condemn corporate prayer. He criticizes praying that is merely for show.

The description of God as unseen in verse 6 may seem out of place in this context. What does God's hiddenness have to do with our praying? Yet, it seems fitting that those who address God, who does his work while unseen, should not draw attention to themselves solely to be noticed by others. This was Christ's pattern as well. Although he carried out a public ministry, Jesus did not go out of his way to make a great noise about himself. He sometimes told those he healed not to tell others about what had happened to them (Matthew 8:4; Mark 3:12). He refused to defend himself to Pilate (Matthew 21:27; Mark 11:33; 15:4). When the people wanted to make him king by force, Jesus withdrew from the crowd (John 6:15). This was partly due to the unique nature of Christ's first coming. These measures were meant to ensure that he would reach Calvary's cross, but these actions also reflected a fundamental humility that is a divine characteristic.

Jesus's warning is an implicit acknowledgment that those who engage in spiritual grandstanding often hope to attract God's attention with their spiritual histrionics. By emphasizing the Father's invisibility, Jesus also points to his omnipresence. The invisible and omnipresent God, who sees all that is done in secret, can also hear what we say in secret. We already have his full attention. We do not need to shout or put on a performance.

Jesus's warning seems especially pertinent in an age where everyone is a brand, and our spiritual heroes are often celebrities. The prominent role that social media has in our daily lives has added a whole new dimension to Jesus's warning about the danger of practicing your righteousness in front of others to be seen by them (Matthew 6:1). Forums like Facebook and Twitter have become venues where we put our spiritual practices on display. This isn't necessarily bad, any more than it is necessarily wrong to stand in the assembly to pray or pray in a public setting. The use of plural pronouns ("our Father," "our daily bread," "our debts," "our debtors," "forgive us," "lead us," "deliver us") in the Lord's Prayer suggests that it was designed to be prayed in public worship. However, the culture of social media is one that makes us highly sensitive to being on public display. Social media can be a forum where users connect with those who share similar values or exchange different ideas. Or it can be a place where the main goal is to pursue "views" and "likes." It does not take much for a post about spiritual practices to disintegrate into a form of spiritualized virtue signaling.

The other danger Jesus warned about was the possibility that we might try to manipulate God with our prayers. This is what the pagans do. They "keep on babbling" in the hope that "they will be heard because of their many words" (Matthew 6:7). Like the previous warning, the problem here is not merely that certain words or prayers are repeated. It seems clear that Jesus intended his disciples to recite the Lord's Prayer. Likewise, the Psalms are full of repeated words and phrases. The error Jesus targets is a problem of empty repetition. Repetition is often meaningful. We sing the same songs repeatedly in worship, not only because the words are meaningful to us but because the act of repetition makes them meaningful. But the pagan approach to prayer had more in common with magic than worship. The priests of Baal called upon the name of Baal from morning until noon and danced around the altar. When Baal did not respond, they cut themselves (1 Kings 18:25–29). In Ephesus, the crowd in the theater shouted: "Great is Artemis of the Ephesians" for two hours (Acts 19:28).

Jesus's warning may have special relevance for those who recite the Lord's Prayer verbatim. Some wrongly assume they can influence God simply by repeating the words of this prayer over and over. Usually, this kind of praying is viewed as a form of penance. It is an approach that reduces prayer to punishment. Yet even devotional repetition may be emptied of its meaning when it becomes rote and mechanical. Repetition can also be a symptom of anxiety. The priests of Baal were agitated because they saw no response to their cries. We can become anxious too when God's response does not fit the timetable we have set for him. Our praying turns to nagging, as we attempt to badger God into action. Jesus's assurance puts us at rest: "Do not be like them, for your Father knows what you need before you ask him." God does not need our reminder.

How long is enough? According to John Calvin, the right answer is as long as it takes to help us: "Anyone who is persuaded that God not only cares for us, but also knows our necessities and anticipates our prayers and our worries before He is told of them, this man will forget his long-windedness and will be content if he makes his prayers as long as it helps the practice of his faith."[7]

A Pattern to Follow

There is evidence as early as the second century that the church also used the Lord's Prayer as a template for their own praying. Tertullian viewed it as a foundation that we can build upon with petitions of our own.[8] Christ's prayer begins with what most of us would consider praise by identifying God as Father and asking both that his name would be set apart as holy and for the coming of God's kingdom. These first two petitions echo the Jewish Kaddish:

> Exalted and hallowed be his great name
> In the world which he created according
>   to his will.
> May he let his kingdom rule
> In your lifetime and in your days and in
>   the lifetime
> Of the whole house of Israel, speedily and
>   soon.
> And to this, say: amen.[9]

The first move, then, in all prayer is a move in God's direction. Prayer begins by recognizing who God really is and what kind of relationship we have with him. Jesus's prayer teaches us that we are not only approaching God as the creator and sovereign of the universe but as our great caregiver. The designation of God as our "Father in Heaven" unites these two ideas. As we will soon see in verse 10, heaven is the place where God's will is always done. Earth is God's domain as much as heaven is, but to speak of God as our heavenly Father is a reminder that we are addressing our creator and the one who is really in control. "Our God is in heaven; he does whatever pleases him," Psalm 115:3 declares.

At the same time, Jesus grants us permission to address this powerful creator on the most intimate terms. Not only is he "Father," in the sense that he is the creator, but Jesus's prayer teaches us to approach God as *our* Father. Prayer as Jesus models it is personal. We are not approaching God as if he is a king who operates at a great distance from us. We are not mere commoners vying with others of greater importance for a small slice of his attention. This is a family matter. Jesus has already told us why this should encourage us. Because he is your Father, God's eyes are upon you. Your Father sees, hears, and cares for you. Unlike someone who petitions royalty and must convince them that they share the same interests, God is already interested in you.

The request that God's name be regarded as holy invites an obvious question. By whom? Although it is true that we sometimes take God for granted, this request, like the two that follow, seems to be directed at the world at large. Jesus's prayer assumes that we already recognize the dignity of God's name. In other words, the position we should take as we approach God is of someone who knows who God is and treats him with the reverence that is his due. Coming to God with the familiarity of a child but also with reverence may sound like a contradiction. Many of us come out of worship traditions that are mostly casual. We do not meet in a sanctuary but an auditorium. We do not sing sacred music but songs. We wear jeans and sweatshirts. The atmosphere is chatty and the service informal. The worship leader tells jokes, and a great effort is made to put everyone at ease. These things may not be bad in themselves, but they increase the likelihood that we will forget our place.

The same is true when it comes to prayer. We are so familiar in our approach to God that we slouch into his presence, mumble a few words without thinking, and then go our way. We have a greater sense of gravity when we meet with our supervisor at work or go out on a first date with someone. But somehow, the fact that we are approaching the creator of the universe does not move us. Is it possible that instead of being comfortable, we have grown callous? We can be confident and reverent at the same time. This is the rationale behind some of the gestures and postures that have traditionally been associated with praying. They are intended to be a forceful reminder of the sacred nature of the activity, but they can also become so familiar to us that all the significance is leached from them. Jesus teaches us to begin with a frame of reference rather than a particular posture or gesture. We might think of it as a posture of mind to fit with the kinesics of prayer.

Jesus further emphasizes this frame of thinking in verse 10: "Your kingdom come, your will be done, on earth as it is in heaven." New Testament commentator John Nolland observes that Jesus's reference to the coming of the kingdom does not have parallels in ancient Jewish texts: "But since the coming of (the day) of Yahweh is common OT diction, and the OT looked forward to a time when in some greater sense God would become king, the petition is readily understood as a reformulation in kingdom language of the OT anticipation of the coming of God in judgment and salvation."[10]

Before turning to our personal concerns, Jesus expands our frame of reference so that we may consider those concerns within the larger context of God's plan for the world. There is more to this petition than asking God to look after his own interests, although that is partly what is meant. It is a way of aligning our plans with God's plan. According to Luke 22:28–30, during the Last Supper, Jesus told his disciples: "You are those who have stood by me in my trials. And I confer on you a kingdom, just as my Father conferred one on me, so that you may eat and drink at my table in my kingdom and sit on thrones, judging the twelve tribes of Israel." The kingdom represents our interests as well as the Father's.

This petition also draws a distinction between heaven and earth. God rules over both, but the request implies earth is not yet a place where God's will is always done. Or, at least, it is not a place where the inhabitants are always inclined toward the will of God. On the one hand, this petition reflects a desire to draw the rule of heaven down to earth. The hope of the kingdom is that its arrival will bring heaven and earth into alignment so that God's will is done on earth just as it is in heaven, but it also has the intent of drawing earth up into heaven. Before we begin to address our earthly concerns, Christ invites us to view them from above. When we pray, we are not shouting at God from a great distance in a frantic effort to get his attention and enlist his aid. The coming of the kingdom and the alignment of heaven and earth that will be its result are reminders of our true position. We are in Christ. Paul graphically depicts the implications of this when he says in Ephesians 2:6 that God has "raised us up with Christ and seated us with him in the heavenly realms in Christ Jesus."

God does not treat our earthly concerns with contempt, but he does expect us to approach these lower concerns with a perspective shaped by the view from above. God is in control. He is busy subduing all things for the sake of Christ. We live in the in-between time, seated with Christ but waiting for the consummation of his kingdom. The perspective Jesus describes in this petition is the same as that expressed by the author of Hebrews, who quotes Psalm 8:4–6, which says that God will bring everything into submission "under the feet" of the son of man. We have not yet seen this, "But we do see Jesus, who was made lower than the angels for a little while, now crowned with glory and honor because he suffered death, so that by the grace of God he might taste death for everyone" (Hebrews 2:9).

While our needs often prompt our prayer, to pray as Jesus taught, we must begin with God. This involves more than thinking about his attributes, though that is often an excellent place to start. It means that we must begin with his agenda. God is in control, but praying for God's kingdom and will is more than recognizing that God is in control. Like Jesus in the Garden of Gethsemane, our prayer for God's will to be done is an act of surrender. But also, like Christ's prayer, it is a surrender to hope.

Peter reflected this perspective of hope when he told the people of Jerusalem: "This man was handed over to you by God's deliberate plan and foreknowledge; and you, with the help of wicked men, put him to death by nailing him to the cross" (Acts 2:23). God was not taken by surprise by the evil acts of those who crucified Jesus. They do not get in the way of his ultimate purposes. When the church prayed for Peter and John after their arrest, they expressed this same confidence. After recalling how Jewish and Roman officials had conspired together against Jesus, they confessed: "They did what your power and will had decided beforehand should happen" (Acts 4:28). The alignment that Jesus teaches us to pray for in the Lord's Prayer is also the one that Paul celebrated when he wrote that "in all things God works for the good of those who love him, who have been called according to his purpose" (Romans 8:28). To surrender to God's will in prayer involves more than a recognition of his power. It is an assurance that flows from his goodness and purpose.

"Everything that happens to you, whether good or bad, must first pass muster before your Father's heart," Helmut Thielicke assures us.[11] This is what it means to bring your earthly concerns to a heavenly Father who knows what you need before you ask him. It is to place both your desires and your needs in his hands and accept what he gives back. "He who is reconciled to the Father is also reconciled to his lot," Thielicke explains. "For whomsoever the will of God has lost its terror (and this it has for all who know the Father of Jesus Christ),

for him the darkest night of the valley of life has lost its
specters and it shines with light."[12]

Body and Spirit

With this framework in mind, we are ready to turn to
the particular needs that affect us. And it should not
surprise us that Jesus, who promised that the child who
asks for bread would not receive a stone, teaches us to
begin with bread (see Matthew 7:9). As the language
shifts from "your" to "our," Jesus teaches us to say: "Give
us today our daily bread" (Matthew 6:11). Although he
may have been alluding to Israel's journey through the
wilderness, where they were fed daily by manna that fell
from heaven, it seems likely that Jesus intended this to
be taken literally. In Jesus's day, bread was not a side dish
but the primary staple, especially for the poor. Food is
one of the most basic concerns that we have, though
most of us do not think about it. The fact that we have
full refrigerators and see restaurants on every corner can
dull our awareness of our dependence on God for our
most basic needs.

Scholars have puzzled over Jesus's description of this
bread as daily. The Greek word appears only here. Some
have seen allusions to the manna that fell in the wilderness, while others link it to the shewbread that the
priests placed daily on the table outside the holy of holies

in the tabernacle. Jerome, who translated the Scriptures into Latin and lived in the fourth and fifth centuries, traced the term to an Aramaic word and believed the phrase should be translated "bread for tomorrow." But for him, this pointed forward to the life to come. On the other hand, John Chrysostom, the great preacher of Constantinople who also lived in the fourth and fifth centuries, saw it as a reference to the food that we need today.

Maybe we do not need to separate the two. God's provision of the food we need for today is an assurance that he will take care of us tomorrow. The fact that God cares for the things we need for material life is a token that he will also provide for us in the life to come. In Jesus's teaching about this, he reasoned in the opposite direction. Since our Heavenly Father has been pleased to give us the kingdom, why should we run after these things? If he has provided for our greatest need, God will attend to the small needs as well (Luke 12:22–34).

The petition for bread, then, can be literal and have spiritual significance. We are right to give thanks to God for our food before we eat, but it is just as appropriate to ask God to provide the meal before we sit down at the table. The request for daily bread includes all the other small concerns that occupy our daily lives. All the things we need to live and the means to provide them are of interest to God because he knows that we need them. We could add many other items to the list as well. We pray for our children, our friends, and our schedules. We ask God for help to accomplish the tasks that we have for the day. Sometimes we even pray for the weather. They are not necessities in the technical sense, but they are a concern for us. Because they are our concerns, God is not ashamed to concern himself with them.

As important as our everyday concerns may be, other needs are even more important. Consequently, the trajectory of personal requests in this prayer moves from material to spiritual. In particular, Jesus singles out the two that are the most critical. One is our need for forgiveness. The other is for spiritual protection. In Matthew 6:12 we are taught to pray: "And forgive us our debts, as we also have forgiven our debtors." The comparison mentioned in this verse is unsettling. Is it a condition? Is Jesus suggesting that we should ask God to make his forgiveness conditional on our forgiving others? The warning of verses 14–15 seems to suggest as much, but to say it this way makes the request sound like bargaining. What is more, we can think of many occasions where we have not forgiven others. From grudges for little slights to outright blame for major transgressions, there is plenty of evidence that shows that forgiveness does not come easily to us. We have no grounds for basing our request that God forgive us on our own track record of forgiveness.

There is even less ground for viewing the "as" in Christ's petition as a matter of degree, as if we were asking God to forgive us to the same extent that we have forgiven others. We try to forgive, but we do not always forgive well. The offenses of others keep coming to mind. Even when we do not punish, we *remember*. If anything, this petition seems intended to bring to mind our penchant for unforgiveness instead of serving as a reason for God to grant us the forgiveness we need. The recognition that we require forgiveness forces us to admit that we must also forgive others. "The word 'as' (in 'as we forgive') does not imply a comparison; how could Jesus's disciples compare their poor forgiving with God's mercy?" Joachim Jeremias explains. "Rather, the 'as' introduces a declaration, for, as we have already seen, the correct translation from the Aramaic must be, 'as we also herewith forgive our debtors.'"[13] If Jeremias is right, our awareness of the need to be forgiven prompts a recognition that we also need to forgive those who have committed offenses against us. This is, in essence, what the king in the parable of the unforgiving servant said should be the case: "'You wicked servant,' he said, 'I canceled all that debt of yours because you begged me to. Shouldn't you have had mercy on your fellow servant just as I had on you?'" (Matthew 18:32).

The petition for spiritual protection in Matthew 6:13 addresses our practice of sin at its point of entrance: "And lead us not into temptation, but deliver us from the evil one." The nature of the request is simple enough. It asks God to keep us out of temptation's way. This strategy is preemptive. Do not even let us come to the place where we feel the enticement to transgress in the first place.

The phrase "lead us not" seems surprising. What does God have to do with temptation? Scripture emphatically denies that God has a role in tempting anyone to evil. It is Satan who is called "the tempter" (Matthew 4:3; 1 Thessalonians 3:5). Furthermore, James 1:13–14 reveals that we are also complicit: "When tempted, no one should say, 'God is tempting me.' For God cannot be tempted by evil, nor does he tempt anyone; but each person is tempted when they are dragged away by their own evil desire and enticed."

This was the case in the garden of Eden. Satan was the agent of temptation, but "when the woman saw that the fruit of the tree was good for food and pleasing to the eye, and also desirable for gaining wisdom, she took some and ate it. She also gave some to her husband, who was with her, and he ate it" (Genesis 3:6). Temptation sometimes arises from an external source (Matthew 18:7). Yet, more often than not, we are our own worst enemy. Instead of fleeing temptation, we position ourselves to be enticed by the environments we place ourselves in, the relationships we choose, and the choices we make. When we ask God not to "lead us" into temptation, we are really asking him to protect us from those external and internal influences that work together to produce temptation. With this in mind, the evil spoken of in this petition can easily have a double force. On the one hand, it is a plea that God will protect us from Satan. He is "the evil one" with whom sin ultimately originated. At the same time, it is a request that God would preserve us from all the powers of evil in the larger sense of the word. With this phrase, we confess that our safety is found in God alone.

The doxology included at the end of Matthew 6:13 in some versions does not seem to have been part of Matthew's original text. It is missing from the oldest manuscripts we currently have available, but it is included in the version that appears in the Didache.[14] There is a parallel in 1 Chronicles 29:11 where David declares: "Yours, LORD, is the greatness and the power and the glory and the majesty and the splendor, for everything in heaven and earth is yours. Yours, LORD, is the kingdom; you are exalted as head over all."

Whether or not the doxology was part of the original, it is a fitting way to close. The Lord's Prayer ends with God just as it begins with him. This is what is at the heart of every prayer. When we pray, we focus our attention on God. We remind ourselves of who he is and what he is like. As we approach him, we place ourselves, our concerns, and even our offenses before him. The confidence we have in doing so comes from the fact that it is Jesus Christ who has taught us to pray this way. He is our mentor in prayer. But more than this, he is our passport into God's presence. "Until now you have not asked for anything in my name," he told his disciples in John 16:24. "Ask and you will receive, and your joy will be complete.

Chapter 8

Prayers Without Words

Be still before the Lord, all mankind, because he has roused
himself from his holy dwelling.
—Zechariah 2:13

Some years ago, a friend admitted to me that she couldn't
pray. "I don't know why," she said. "But it's like choking."
She wrote to me recently and said that she still struggles.
"I have read so much on prayer, and it still sticks in my
throat and comes out halting and inadequate." She is not
alone. Some of the godliest people have found themselves
at a loss for words in the presence of God.

Sometimes it is the silence of awe. When Daniel the
prophet was an old man in his eighties, he had a vision
that puzzled him. After fasting for three weeks, he encountered a figure on the banks of the river Tigris dressed in
white linen with a belt of gold. His appearance shown like
lightning, and his eyes were like flaming torches. Daniel's

companions, who could not see the vision but felt his presence, fled in terror. Daniel was so overcome at the sight that he fainted. The heavenly being reached out to touch Daniel and spoke words of encouragement. As Daniel slowly rose, first on his hands and knees and then with trembling on his feet, the man assured him that his prayers had been heard. He had come to explain the vision. "While he was saying this to me," Daniel later wrote, "I bowed with my face toward the ground and was speechless" (Daniel 10:15). When the being touched Daniel's lips, he was finally able to speak. "I am over-come with anguish because of the vision, my lord, and I feel very weak," he said. "How can I, your servant, talk with you, my lord? My strength is gone and I can hardly breathe" (Daniel 10:16–17).

The Sounds of Silence

It is doubtful that many, if any of us, have had an experi-ence like Daniel's. But we have all had moments of awe that took our breath away. The sight of a newborn child, a spectacular sunset, or the sound of a well-loved piece of music can leave us speechless. The same can happen in moments of terror. We are struck dumb with fear. Those who have encountered God sometimes experience a mixture of both. John's encounter with the risen Christ on the island of Patmos strongly echoes what happened to Daniel (Revelation 1:12–17).

Silence is the reaction of those who are perplexed or astonished. God's reply to Job's extensive complaint stunned the patriarch into silence. Job's initial reaction was to say, "I am unworthy—how can I reply to you? I put my hand over my mouth. I spoke once, but I have no answer—twice, but I will say no more" (Job 40:4–5). In prayer, we may come to God but find ourselves so confounded that we do not know what to say. Sometimes this is because we have realized something about God that overwhelms us. Or, as in Job's case, by interacting with God we suddenly realize something about ourselves that leaves us dumbfounded. It may be that we finally understand the flaw in our complaint or recognize the gravity of our fallenness.

Silence is the primary disposition of the learner. Learning can involve speaking, but it usually begins with listening, and listening demands silence from us. In the Old Testament, sacred ceremonies sometimes concluded with a call for silence on the part of God's people (Deuteronomy 27:9; Nehemiah 8:11). The prophets called for silence as divine judgment approached (Habakkuk 2:20; Zephaniah 1:7; Zechariah 2:13). According to Revelation 8:1, there is even silence in heaven.

Silence, Stephen H. Webb, points out is not a natural state. "If we try to hear silence," Webb explains, "we will always hear something making noise instead."[1] Likewise, silence is not the usual state of those who pray.

Indeed, it seems to be the very antithesis of prayer. Yet silence in God's presence does not have to be a bad thing. Ecclesiastes 3:7 tells us that there is a time to be silent and a time to speak. The same writer counsels those who go to the house of God to be measured in their words: "Guard your steps when you go to the house of God. Go near to listen rather than to offer the sacrifice of fools, who do not know that they do wrong. Do not be quick with your mouth, do not be hasty in your heart to utter anything before God. God is in heaven and you are on earth, so let your words be few" (Ecclesiastes 5:1–2).

We might have expected the writer to tell us to watch our words. Instead, he equates our words with our ways. There is more going on here than a warning about our deportment or the formal way we address God in prayer. He is not merely saying, "Mind your manners." We are warned that when we approach God, we must have a sense of God's presence as well as a sense of our place before him. It is easy to be careless in our worship and our praying. We are absent-minded, too quick to offer empty words and cheap promises. Frequently, this is because we are speaking out of habit. We are saying the things we have always said without considering whether we actually mean them.

When the writer of Ecclesiastes warns about the danger of making rash vows, he is talking about more than the temptation to make promises that we cannot keep. He is reminding us that we often try to manipulate God with our speech. His caution is similar to the one that Jesus gave when he told his disciples not to think that they could pressure God by piling up words (Matthew 6:7). Or else we may try to bargain with God, attempting to negotiate the answers to our prayers by making promises. They may be sincere but out of reach. This is the kind of commitment that looks only at the expected benefit but not the terms. We are so eager for the answer that we do not consider the impossibility of what we are saying. Or it is a calculated promise with loopholes, like the Pharisees who declared they might have used their money or property to help their parents as being "devoted to God" so that they could use it for themselves instead (Mark 7:9–12).

There is good reason to tread carefully when we approach God. It is not because he is irascible and easily angered. We all know hypersensitive people before whom we must weigh our words. We walk on eggshells whenever we talk to them because we are not sure how they will respond. This is not the issue with God; the problem is with us. We are the ones who are flighty and rash. We take God for granted. We babble and chatter because we feel we must say something but have not thought about what we ought to say. We are not self-aware, nor are we much aware of God either. "If you have to go to the temple like an imbecile, who goes because the others do it, or like a fool, who would as soon do that as something else, it is not worth doing," Jacques Ellul explains. "Reflect, then, before you approach the place where God is adored, the place where he may speak. Watch your step. Try to be aware of what you are doing."[2]

These warnings do not minimize the importance of words but the opposite. They assume their gravity. The writer of Ecclesiastes warns us to be sparing in our words because words mean something. If there is a danger in thoughtless prayer, it is that God might take us at our word and deal with us as we have asked. It is no accident that the Hebrew term for "word" can also be translated "deed." God is not cavalier about the words he chooses. He means what he says. There are no empty words with God. It is reasonable that he should expect the same from us. Our dilemma in prayer is the same as Isaiah's: "I am a man of unclean lips, and I live among a people of unclean lips" (Isaiah 6:5). It is good to begin in silence and ask God to help us weigh our words before we open our mouths.

Silence as an Act of Faith

We often mistake silence for emptiness. We are afraid of emptiness. That is why we tend to chatter when there is a prolonged break in a conversation. We feel compelled to fill the void with something. Anything. God views silence differently. We have already observed that God is comfortable with his own silence. He is no chatterbox. There is much that God has said. There is even more that he has not. God is equally comfortable with our silence; sometimes he prefers it.

After Moses was told that he would not be permitted to go into the land of promise with Israel, he prayed an earnest prayer and begged God to reconsider. It is easy to see why. Moses had gone through many trials and sacrificed much to get to this point. It is no wonder that the Bible says that Moses pleaded with God (Deuteronomy 3:23). Three features of his prayer stand out. One is its brevity. Despite its strong feeling, it is only a short prayer with a single request: "Let me go over and see the good land beyond the Jordan—that fine hill country and Lebanon" (v. 25). Perhaps Moses said more that was not recorded, but the essence of the request was brief. Moses asked only to be able to see the land. He didn't even ask to live there.

The second notable feature of his prayer is the basis for his request. Moses did not argue that God should allow him to see the land because of all his effort. He did not say, "Look at all I have done for you! You owe me this." Nor did Moses suggest that God should grant his request since he had been mostly obedient. Instead, Moses based his appeal on God himself: "Sovereign LORD, you have begun to show to your servant your greatness and your strong hand. For what god is there in heaven or on earth who can do the deeds and mighty works you do?" (v. 24).

This was not flattery. Moses was not trying to get on God's good side by saying nice things about him. This appeal to grace makes the prayer's third feature all the more striking. It is God's terse response: "'That is enough,' the LORD said. 'Do not speak to me anymore about this matter'" (v. 26). What is meant by "enough"? Does God mean, "That is enough complaining?" Is he saying, "You have asked me enough times about this?" Or is it possible that he meant that what Moses had seen was already sufficient? After all, Moses had seen God's glory. What more could there be for him to see after that?

Moses gives the rationale for God's refusal when he explains to Israel, "Because of you the LORD was angry with me and would not listen to me" (Deuteronomy 3:26). However, this was only part of the story. Later in Deuteronomy, Moses reveals that he was not allowed to enter the land because he and Aaron broke faith when they failed to uphold God's holiness at Meribah Kadesh in the desert of Zin. In anger, Moses struck the rock instead of speaking to it as commanded. "Listen, you rebels, must we bring you water out of this rock?" he said, appearing to take partial credit for the miracle that followed (Numbers 20:6–11).

Some commentators hear an echo of God's reply to Moses when Paul writes of God's answer to his plea to be delivered from his thorn in his flesh. The apostle does not reveal this thorn's exact nature, only that it was a "messenger of Satan" sent to torment him and keep him from becoming conceited (2 Corinthians 12:7). Paul begged the Lord three times to remove the thorn. Instead, God said, "My grace is sufficient for you, for my power is made perfect in weakness" (2 Corinthians 12:9). God's grace is always enough.

Although God's answer to both prayers was essentially the same, the context was quite different. Moses was refused because he had disobeyed God's command and had failed to show reverence to him. Paul's request was denied for a different reason. God allowed the thorn to keep the apostle from becoming conceited from the "surpassingly great revelations" that he had received (2 Corinthians 12:7). These two examples show some of the reasons we don't see the results from our prayers that we would like. Sometimes it is because of actions we have taken. Like Moses, we ask God to remove the consequences of our choices. Instead, he calls us to be obedient to him in the midst of them. At other times, we are praying about things that are the result of choices that others make. We don't have control over their decisions or our circumstances. We must trust God to work things out in our best interest despite the choices that others make. Or, as in Paul's case, there is nobody to blame. God says no simply because the thing we have requested does not fall along the path he has chosen for us.

All these situations essentially call for the same response. Silence does not always mean that we do not have words to say. Sometimes silence is an act of faith. We do not speak because we are at rest. What was true for Paul was equally true for Moses. It is also true for us. God's grace is enough, even when the answer to our prayers turns out to be a profound disappointment. Even though God turned down his request, Moses's confidence in his grace was not misplaced. The Lord refused to allow Moses to enter the land, but he did enable him to see it "from a distance" (Deuteronomy 32:52).

Another group of people praying in silence are those who are waiting. The silence they bring into God's presence may be a silence born of expectation. When Moses was not allowed to see the fulfillment of his lifelong dream, he joined a large company of faithful believers whose desires were not granted in this life because God had something better planned. Abraham, Moses, Isaac, and Jacob all died without receiving the inheritance that

God had promised to them. "All these people were still living by faith when they died," Hebrews 11:13 observes. "They did not receive the things promised; they only saw them and welcomed them from a distance, admitting that they were foreigners and strangers on earth." The promise did not fail. Their time had not yet come. Along with them are countless others who were tortured, jeered, and flogged. They were destitute, persecuted, mistreated, and eventually put to death. "These were all commended for their faith, yet none of them received what had been promised," the writer of Hebrews explains, "since God had planned something better for us so that only together with us would they be made perfect" (Hebrews 11:39–40).

Like them, the answers to our prayers are bound up with the plans that God has for others. We do not have to understand why God has not done what we have asked to trust that his plans are better than our dreams. The silence we bring with us to prayer may sometimes express disappointment, or it can express the assurance of our faith as we anticipate and long for God's promises from a distance.

Groans, Sighs, and Cries

A popular Christian song of an earlier era says that tears are a language that God understands. Apparently, he also understands sighs, groans, and even roars. Job and the Psalms describe a vocabulary of prayer that includes inarticulate cries of grief, longing, and pain. "Why is life given to a man whose way is hidden, whom God has hedged in?" Job complains. "For sighing has become my daily food; my groans pour out like water" (Job 3:23–24). Job did not keep these inarticulate complaints to himself. He expressed them to God in a language that went beyond words (Job 23:2). Likewise, in Psalm 38:9, David says, "All my longings lie open before you, Lord; my sighing is not hidden from you." This is not the soft sigh of one who is content but a cry of deep sorrow or physical distress. In this same psalm, David says, "I am feeble and utterly crushed; I groan in anguish of heart" (Psalm 38:8). The Hebrew word that is translated "groan" in this verse speaks of a loud cry. It is the same one that appears in Psalm 22:1, which was quoted in part by Jesus on the cross: "Why are you so far from saving me, so far from my cries of anguish?" The Gospels say that Jesus cried out in a loud voice on the cross (Matthew 27:46, 50; Mark 15:34, 37; Luke 23:46).

There are times when we have no words to offer God, only our strangled cries of anguish. Sometimes this is because the pain we feel is so great that it drives all thought from our minds. Even if we tried, we would not be able to formulate the sentences. Our groans are not metaphorical; they are literal. At other times, it is because we do not know what to say. We are confounded. We only know how we feel. Fortunately, we are not limited to words when it comes to prayer. What we are unable to say in a sentence can be expressed in a sob or a moan. The frequency with which Scripture mentions tears proves that they really are a language that God understands. The One who wept at the tomb of Lazarus will not look down on our groans, sighs, and tears.

When those we care about are experiencing pain or trauma, it can be tempting to address the problem with a sentiment. We speak to them about God's care in cliches and platitudes. We may minimize their suffering by trying to persuade them that things are not as bad as they seem. Or we dismiss the pain by pointing to some blessing that God has in store because of it. One reason for this is because their suffering causes us discomfort. We cannot deny that it exists, but we would prefer not to dwell on it. We want them to feel better, so we hurry past their pain in a vain effort to move them toward joy. We rarely find it helpful when we are on the receiving end of this kind of comfort, but we may not realize that we can treat ourselves the same way when it comes to prayer. We may rush past our pain and speak in platitudes instead. Whether this is because we do not have a vocabulary that is adequate to express our pain or do not think it is appropriate to speak to God of such things, the result is the same. We draw little comfort from these prayers. The guttural cries of Scripture are permission to address God differently. If you cannot find the words, then speak to God in sighs. If sighs are not enough, then offer up your cries and groans instead. Groans are a language that God understands too.

God understands groans because it is a language that he speaks. According to Romans 8:26, "The Spirit himself intercedes for us through wordless groans." Paul says that the Spirit does this because we do not know what to say. When we find ourselves at a loss for words in God's presence, we can take comfort in the knowledge that the Spirit is praying for us. This mysterious promise has puzzled believers. Some interpret it as a reference to glossolalia or what is commonly known as speaking in tongues. Undoubtedly, the gift of tongues was an example of the Holy Spirit speaking through the believer. But the fact that Paul characterizes the Spirit's communication as *wordless* makes it unlikely that he has tongues in view. Those who spoke in tongues spoke languages. On the day of Pentecost, the crowd made up of people from many nations heard the disciples declaring God's wonders in their own languages (Acts 2:11). When Paul provided guidelines for the exercise of the gift of tongues in the Corinthian church, it is equally clear that some form of language was in view. Otherwise, there would have been no need for an interpreter to be present (1 Corinthians 14:13, 27).

The communication of the Spirit in Romans 8:26 is wordless in the sense that the person who prays does not hear it. God, however, knows what the Spirit has in mind for us. Although we can always be sure that God hears our prayers, we cannot always be certain that he will grant our requests. We do not always know whether our desires fit into God's plans. "We are often in the position of a child who wants something which would be bound only to hurt him," William Barclay observes, "and God is often in the position of a parent who has to refuse his child's request or compel him to do something he does not want to do, because he knows what is to the child's good far better than the child himself."[3]

This is not an issue when the Holy Spirit prays. Because the Spirit knows the Father's mind, his requests always agree with God's will. Since this is a prerequisite to answered prayer, we can be certain that whatever the Spirit asks on our behalf will be granted (1 John 5:15). We do not need to know the specific nature of his requests to know that they are good for us.

What Paul describes may sound mechanical, like an operation that works in the background entirely apart from our involvement. Perhaps Paul is only arguing from the lesser to the greater, noting that a God who knows what is in our hearts must also know the mind of the Spirit. Yet he seems to make a direct connection between the Spirit's intercession and the working of our hearts when he says that "he who searches our hearts knows the mind of the Spirit, because the Spirit intercedes for God's people in accordance with the will of God" (Romans 8:27). This particular working of the Spirit is not independent of us. It is not a side conversation. The apostle's language of personal engagement links the Father's understanding of what the Spirit asks with his act of searching our hearts, suggesting that the two are simultaneous. God discerns the mind of the Spirit by searching our hearts.

The Spirit functions not only as our intercessor but as our proxy. When we don't know how to pray, he takes the deep desires of our hearts and reframes them in a way that corresponds with the Father's will. In this way, the Spirit's wordless intercession becomes our prayer as well. As the Spirit prays for the believer, the believer also prays through the Spirit. Theologian Herman Ridderbos explains, "He unites himself with their prayer, so that their prayer becomes his prayer, and that which they cannot utter is judged by God, who searches the hearts, according to the intention of the Spirit (Romans 8:27)."[4]

The Spirit is not alone in his work. Paul goes on in this chapter to point out that Jesus Christ is "at the right hand of God and is also interceding for us" (Romans 8:34). We are tempted to think of our prayers as feeble things. They are only a puff of breath filled with the confused longings of our hearts. We do not know what to say. We are not sure whether God will give us what we want. But Paul paints a very different picture of what is happening. He removes the veil of our struggle to reveal a convergence of Father, Son, and Holy Spirit working together not only in response to our prayers but to help us pray.

Why Are You Crying Out to Me?

Most people would probably say that they don't pray enough, but our best times of prayer may be found in our actions. Exodus 14 tells how the Israelites panicked when they saw Pharaoh's army coming after them in furious pursuit. "Was it because there were no graves in Egypt that you brought us to the desert to die?" they complained. "What have you done to us by bringing us out of Egypt? Didn't we say to you in Egypt, 'Leave us alone; let us serve the Egyptians'? It would have been better for us to serve the Egyptians than to die in the desert!" (Exodus 14:11–12).

Moses urged them to stand firm. "The LORD will fight for you," he said. "You need only to be still" (Exodus 14:14). In other words, Moses told them to pipe down and wait for God's deliverance. But Moses was not quiet. The Lord's response in verse 15 implies that Moses was praying. The Lord said to Moses, "Why are you crying out to me? Tell the Israelites to move on." The sort of prayer spoken of in this verse is the kind we pray in desperation. It is a cry of fear. Perhaps the Lord was speaking to Moses as the representative of his people. It is the same word used in verse 10 to describe Israel's terrified prayer when they saw the Egyptians marching after them. Moses certainly did not seem afraid when he told the people to stand firm and wait for the deliverance of the Lord. "The Egyptians you see today you will never see again," he declared (v. 13).

Either way, God's response is not what we would expect. It is a good reminder that prayer and action are compatible with each other. We do not have to choose between them. It is possible to pray and act at the same time. In some cases, action is our best prayer. If offering our bodies as a living sacrifice is true and proper worship, then consecrated action is itself a kind of language. There are times when we employ prayer as a strategy for procrastination. We hide our lack of resolve and fear under a cloak of spirituality. We hope that God will resolve the problem without us having to do anything. In a way, this was the course of action that Moses had proposed, although it is possible that he was only speaking figuratively and actually meant something like, "Stand firm in your faith." God had a different strategy in mind. Moses said, "Stand still," but God's command was to "move on."

Although actions may not be prayer in a technical sense, it is a language we use to express our faith to God (James 2:18). How, then, do we know when action is needed instead of prayer? As with Israel, it is often the situation that determines this. In Israel's case, there was only one direction for them to go. We frequently find ourselves in the same place—not pinned against the sea with enemies at our back, but in contexts where the course of action that God wants us to take is so obvious that we don't need to pray about it. I do not need to pray about loving my spouse, doing my job well, or treating my neighbor with respect. I may want to ask God to show me the best way to do these things, but much of the time, the path set before me is so evident that common sense is all that is required. Where God has given a clear command in Scripture, we do not need to pray about whether it is his will for us to obey. Where he has not provided clear instruction, in the majority of cases, circumstances will reveal what needs to be done.

But what about those situations that fall in between these two extremes? I am talking about those times when the options before us don't involve a clear mandate from Scripture and our circumstances don't dictate a straightforward course of action. We have prayed and yet have no sense from God that he prefers one path over the other. If time and circumstances allow, we can certainly wait and continue seeking direction from God. In such instances, the best rule may be: "When in doubt ... don't." But there are also times when we *must* make a decision. In these cases, the best rule is to follow the path that appeals to you the most until God directs you to do otherwise.

Does God's seeming lack of response in such situations indicate that he does not care which course we choose? In some cases, perhaps. God probably doesn't care whether you wear red or blue today. But if it is true, as Paul declares in Philippians 2:13, that "it is God who works in you to will and to act in order to fulfill his good purpose," then we should not be surprised to find that our inclination often aligns with his without having to be told. This does not mean that we always want to do what God wants us to do. Jesus's prayer in the garden is proof enough that it is possible for us to have a will that deviates from the path that God has laid out for us. But if God has not made a particular path clear to us by Scripture, circumstance, or impulse of the Spirit, we should not be afraid to follow our inclinations. God is able to redirect us. We do not need to hear a voice from heaven. We do not always need to fast and pray to know what to do next.

Silence seems incompatible with prayer. But lovers know that they do not need to talk all the time to enjoy each other's company. Silence may signal confusion, but it can also be a mark of contentment. As the hymn writer Isaac Watts observed in his paraphrase of Psalm 23:

> The sure provisions of my God
>   attend me all my days;
> oh, may your house be mine abode,
>   and all my work be praise.
> There would I find a settled rest,
>   while others go and come;
> no more a stranger, nor a guest,
>   but like a child at home.[5]

If you don't know what to say when you come into God's presence, then say nothing. You are neither a stranger nor a guest. You are God's child. And because of that, you are always welcome.

Chapter 9

Faith, Hope, and Prayer

Faith is reason at rest in God.
—*Charles Haddon Spurgeon*

It is impossible to talk about prayer without also talking about faith and doubt. The two are bound up with prayer in Scripture. The extreme ends of our struggle in this area are reflected in the extravagant promises of Jesus and in James's sober warning. Jesus emphasized faith's potential to a seemingly limitless degree. When the disciples marveled that Jesus had caused a fig tree to wither with only a few words, he told them to have faith in God. "Truly I tell you, if anyone says to this mountain, 'Go, throw yourself into the sea,' and does not doubt in their heart but believes that what they say will happen, it will be done for them," Jesus said. "Therefore I tell you, whatever you ask for in prayer, believe that you have received it, and it will be yours" (Mark 11:22–23).

James looks at the prospect of answered prayer from a different angle. Instead of focusing on what God can do through faith, he warns of the undermining effect of doubt. "If any of you lacks wisdom, you should ask God, who gives generously to all without finding fault, and it will be given to you," he assures. "But when you ask, you must believe and not doubt, because the one who doubts is like a wave of the sea, blown and tossed by the wind. That person should not expect to receive anything from the Lord" (James 1:6–7). James calls the person who doubts double-minded and unstable.

I feel caught between these two Scriptures. On the one hand, as encouraging as the promise of Jesus is to me, it creates an expectation for the results of prayer that does not seem to match my experience. This does not shake my trust in God so much as it erodes the confidence I have in my faith. Jesus's promise seems to place pressure on the outcome of my praying. I review the answers to my prayers, trying to determine whether they rise to the standard of Christ's "whatever you ask for." Does the fact that they do not mean that my faith was deficient? It is a little like investors who read the quarterly statement and second-guess their choices. Would the answers have been better if I had prayed differently?

If Jesus's promise causes me to question my prayers after the fact, the warning of James 1:6–7 makes me worry about them at the outset. James seems absolute. If you doubt, don't expect to receive anything from God. But if by doubt, he means someone who sometimes wonders whether God is going to grant their request, then I am afraid that I am often guilty. Jesus's promise may lead me to have unrealistic expectations of God, and James makes it sound like God has unreasonable expectations of me. Either way, it is hard for me to come to prayer without a certain amount of doubt.

Have Faith in God

My problem on both sides of this equation is that I have put the wrong figure at the center. In either instance, I think that my prayer's answer is more dependent upon me than it is upon God. This is certainly not where Jesus begins. His primary assertion is not "trust in your faith" but "have faith in God." Prayer's vast potential springs from a faith that is placed in God. The "whatever" potential of prayer is not because the one who prays has the potential to accomplish whatever he or she might want but because God can do whatever he pleases (Job 23:13; Psalm 115:3).

Faith is the foundation of all that we do in the Christian life. Our Christian life begins in faith when we receive the righteousness of Christ as a gift by faith. As Paul explains in Romans 1:17, it is "a righteousness that is by faith from first to last." The Greek text literally says that God's righteousness is revealed "out of faith into faith." Whether it is our righteousness of position or practice, the righteousness spoken of in the gospel is "a righteous status which is altogether by faith."[1] Or, as New Testament scholar C. K. Barrett points out, in this verse, Paul "is again emphasizing the principle of 'faith all the time': man (if righteous at all) is righteous by faith; he also lives by faith."[2]

By way of contrast, we tend to emphasize the importance of faith at the beginning of our Christian experience and then leave it there. The result is that we preach faith to the unbeliever and effort to the believer. This can affect the way we look at faith in connection with prayer. We may think of faith as a kind of spiritual energy that we must stir up within ourselves to get the answers we want. The greater the request, the more energy we need. Or we come to view the faith associated with prayer as an ineffable quality of emotion. To get the right answer, we need to muster up a certain kind of feeling that the Bible defines as faith.

This is certainly not how faith works in salvation. Saving faith is a conviction that God can do for us through Christ what we cannot do for ourselves. It is a confidence in God's power and willingness to save, not an emotional state. We are not saved because we feel something about God to a certain degree. We are saved because we believe that he has saved us through his Son. No doubt, feelings will follow. As John says, "We love because he first loved us" (1 John 4:19). But the strong feelings of love toward God that we experience are a consequence, not the cause, of our salvation.

Faith works the same way when it comes to prayer. It is not an emotional state but a conviction about what God is both able and willing to do if we ask him. Yet it is only fair to note that it is Jesus himself who seems to suggest that uncertainty is a deal breaker when it comes to prayer. He qualifies his promise with an exception: "Truly I tell you, if anyone says to this mountain, 'Go, throw yourself into the sea,' and does not doubt in their heart but believes that what they say will happen, it will be done for them" (Mark 11:23). The clause "and does not doubt" sounds as if absolute certainty is a prerequisite for answers to prayer. Confidence that God will hear my request and respond as he deems best is one thing. Certainty that I will get what I ask is something else. If this is what the Bible means by faith, then I may as well not bother. Many, if not most, of my prayers, have an element of uncertainty to them. I have often prayed with conviction and hope but without knowing the outcome. I have prayed for jobs I was not sure I would get and healing that I could not be sure would take place.

I did not always get the answer I wanted. I have prayed for decades for the salvation of family members who are still living in unbelief. I do not yet know what the outcome of those prayers will be.

The perception that we need to be sure in advance that we will get precisely what we ask for has caused many people anxiety. There is a difference between confidence that God will answer my prayer and certainty about the way it will be answered. Jesus urges us to pray with confidence. This does not mean we can always know how God will answer our prayers or that we will always get what we desire. We need go no further than Jesus's own prayer to prove that faith in prayer is not synonymous with the certainty of its outcome. In Gethsemane, Jesus framed his request in language that affirmed his faith without expressing certainty about the result: "'Abba, Father,' he said, 'everything is possible for you. Take this cup from me. Yet not what I will, but what you will'" (Mark 14:36).

On the one hand, Jesus addressed the Father with intimacy and conviction. At the same time, Jesus stated his petition in a way that allowed the Father to refuse. All things are possible with Abba, but this particular request may fall outside his Father's will. In this way, Jesus's prayer in the garden is much like our own. We are not wavering in our faith when we express uncertainty over the outcome, but we acknowledge that we are limited in our perspective. We know that God can do as we ask, but we want him to do what is right and best.

Degrees of Faith

However, there are times when our faith does waver. Perhaps it is the nature of the request that gives us pause. We are overwhelmed by the problem and have difficulty seeing a solution. Or it may be a concern that is so long-standing that we have begun to lose hope. I admire the heroes of faith in church history and Scripture, but the father's prayer in Mark 9 resonates most with my own. Ever since childhood, his son had been possessed by a spirit that robbed him of speech and sent him into convulsions. When Jesus asked the man how long his son had been like this, he told him it had been since childhood. "'It has often thrown him into fire or water to kill him. But if you can do anything, take pity on us and help us.'"If you can"?' said Jesus. 'Everything is possible for one who believes'" (Mark 9:21–22).

Jesus rebuked the father for his lack of faith, but what was the nature of the faith that Jesus expected? The man's weakness was his view of Jesus. "If you can," the man had said. He questioned Jesus's ability to do what was asked. In turn, Jesus demanded faith at the focal point of his doubt. He called upon the man to believe, not so much in the possibility of healing, but in him.

The father responded with honesty. The fact that he had come to Jesus with his son in the first place indicates that he possessed a measure of faith, but like the doubter of James 1:8, he was of two minds in the matter. Jesus's tone may seem unnecessarily harsh, but the father's response shows that it had the intended effect. Instead of turning inward to try and find more faith, the father looks to Jesus for help. "Immediately the boy's father exclaimed, 'I do believe; help me overcome my unbelief!'" (Mark 9:24). Jesus did not speak this way to the boy's father to humiliate him but to open his eyes to the nature of the problem. To find a solution, this father must go all the way and cast his hope entirely on Jesus. Christ is the remedy, not only for the man's son but for the father as well. This was Jesus's pattern with all who were weak in faith. He did not drive them away but challenged them to press in further.

We can see this in those Jesus commended as examples of faith. He does not praise them because they are certain of the outcome of their request but because of their conviction about Christ. Jesus marveled at the Roman centurion in Matthew 8:5–13 not only because he believed his servant would be healed but because the centurion had grasped who Jesus was. "Lord, I do not deserve to have you come under my roof. But just say the word, and my servant will be healed," the centurion said.

"For I myself am a man under authority, with soldiers under me. I tell this one, 'Go,' and he goes; and that one, 'Come,' and he comes. I say to my servant, 'Do this,' and he does it." The centurion expressed a conviction about what Jesus was able to do, but even more, he proclaimed his identity by calling him Lord.

New Testament scholar Joachim Jeremias suggests that Jesus's first response to the centurion should be seen as a refusal: "Matthew 8:7 is to be read as a negative answer in the form of a question: 'Am I to come (into your home, an unclean Gentile) and make him (your servant) healthy?'" He explains, "Jesus is not saying that he is ready to come; on the contrary, he is refusing help."[3] Instead of trying to persuade Jesus to go with him, the centurion "indicates that his confidence in Jesus's power and will to help is unshakable."[4] As Jeremias explains, the force of the centurion's statement is that if he, as an insignificant man, can give orders to his soldiers so that they carry them out, how much more can Jesus heal his paralyzed servant?

Similarly, Jesus commended the Syrophoenician woman's faith in Mark 7 for refusing to take no for an answer when he initially declined her request to drive a demon out of her daughter. "'First let the children eat all they want,' he told her, 'for it is not right to take the children's bread and toss it to the dogs'" (Mark 7:27).

Jesus's answer is not the rejection that it may seem at first glance. He did not refuse absolutely but instead stressed the priority of his ministry to the children of Israel. As Israel's promised Messiah, he had come to the Jew first (see Romans 1:16; 2:9–10). The woman's reaction shows a combination of humility and confidence. She accepts Jesus's assertion that the children have priority but persists in her appeal. "Lord," she replied, "even the dogs under the table eat the children's crumbs" (Mark 7:28). Like the centurion, Jesus praises her for her "great faith" (Matthew 15:28). And like the centurion's servant, Jesus heals her daughter from a distance. Jeremias explains that both stories "show clearly that the attitude of both these Gentiles who sought for help embraced more than superstitious hope for a miracle."[5]

Although the Syrophoenician woman and the centurion both come to Jesus confident that he can grant their request, their expectation is directed at something more than the petition itself. Their faith is focused on Jesus. They believe that Jesus has the power, but they also believe that he will help. Instead of turning their gaze inward to ascertain whether they have enough faith to warrant an answer to their request, they concentrate on Christ.

Jesus's words of praise for the centurion in Matthew 8:10 that he had "not found anyone in Israel with such great faith" is a reminder that some have more faith than others. Faith is a gift as well as a command. Because it is a gift, not everyone has faith in the same proportion. Some, like the centurion, seem to have great faith. We read their biographies and wish we could be like them. But "you of little faith," Jesus's favorite designation for his followers, seems to imply that the opposite is more likely the case (Matthew 6:30; 8:26; 14:31; 16:8; see also Luke 12:28). When Jesus's disciples recognized their limits in this area, they asked Jesus to increase their faith. But instead of offering a regimen of faith-building exercises, he told them, "If you have faith as small as a mustard seed, you can say to this mulberry tree, 'Be uprooted and planted in the sea,' and it will obey you" (Luke 17:6).

Great faith is admirable, but according to Jesus, even a little faith is enough to see remarkable results. Instead of telling them to increase their faith before going to God in prayer, he urges them to begin with the small measure of faith they have. Does this mean that we should be content with meager faith? Jesus is not lowering the bar on faith. He only says that more is possible than we can now imagine. Jesus is more confident of the potential our prayers have than we are. He knows that their outcome is correlated more with the greatness of God than the magnitude of our faith. Jesus also knows that a small faith, once it is exercised, grows larger. But apparently, it is not miracles that cause faith to increase.

The man who asked Jesus to help his unbelief brought his demon-possessed son to the disciples first, and they were unable to help (Mark 9:18). This was *after* Jesus had given them authority over evil spirits and sent them out to preach in the villages in pairs. Mark 6:13 says that at that time, they "drove out many demons and anointed many sick people with oil and healed them." Jesus also chided the disciples for being of little faith when they fretted over their lack of bread after the miracle of the loaves and fish (Mark 8:17–21). Peter is famous for stepping out of the boat during the storm and walking on water. He is just as famous for the panic he felt when he took note of the wind and the water: "Immediately Jesus reached out his hand and caught him. 'You of little faith,' he said, 'why did you doubt?'" (Matthew 14:31).

You would think that our faith would grow in direct proportion to the magnitude of the things that God does as a result of it. Miracles should beget faith. The inconstant faith of the first disciples is proof that this is not the case. It never has been. Deuteronomy 29 describes how the second generation of Israelites renewed the covenant in the land of Moab. At that time, Moses reminded them of all that God had done for them. After forty years of traveling, their clothes and sandals had not worn out. They had lived off food that fell from heaven. They had defeated their enemies when all the odds were against them. "With your own eyes you saw those great trials, those signs and great wonders," he said. "But to this day the LORD has not given you a mind that understands or eyes that see or ears that hear" (Deuteronomy 29:3–4). Despite these experiences, Moses warned that a future generation would forget all this and abandon the covenant (Deuteronomy 29:22–28).

Miracles do not guarantee faith because faith requires more than observing what God has done. It also requires more than a powerful spiritual experience. According to Moses, faith is ultimately an insight that comes from God. It is a mind that understands, eyes that see, and ears that hear. More than a vision of some potential outcome, faith in prayer is grounded in our view of God. This is because faith is trust. The nineteenth-century Scottish preacher John Ker noted, "We can believe a truth, but we can trust only a person,—we can admire a truth, but we can love only a person—we can meditate on a truth, we can commune only with a person, and faith stretches out a wistful hand to touch His garment that it may come at last to embrace Himself."[6] For the Christian, truth is personal, not only because we embrace it as individuals but because it points to the person of Jesus Christ. "You study the Scriptures diligently because you think that in them you have eternal life," Jesus told the religious leaders of his day. "These are the very Scriptures that testify about me, yet you refuse to come to me to have life" (John 5:39–40).

How to Pray with Faith and Hope

This personal dimension of faith explains why Jesus so often seems to attribute the results of his miracles to the faith of those who experience them (Matthew 8:13; 9:22, 29; Mark 10:52; Luke 7:50; 17:19; 18:42). It is not a question of mind over matter. Faith is only as effective as its object. If Jesus were unable or unwilling to respond to my prayers, it would make little difference how much confidence I placed in him. I cannot make him into something he is not by the sheer force of my will. Neither are the results of my faith a reward in the formal sense. The answers to our prayers are not a payment owed to us. Our faith does not gratify God. He does not dole out answers to those who pray because their praise strokes his ego. Christ's statement is relational. It acknowledges the trust others have placed in him. It is a way of saying, "Your faith in me is justified."

But what are we to make of the variation implied in statements like these? Does Jesus do more for some than he does for others because they trust him more? The answer would seem to be a qualified yes. Christ seems to show a kind of deference in this matter. Jesus deals with us according to our expectation. He does not force his way in and overpower us. He says, "According to your faith let it be done to you" (Matthew 9:29). There is a measure of self-fulfillment in this. Those who do not trust Christ also do not turn to him for help and so go unhelped. I do not mean that he ignores them altogether. God "gives everyone life and breath and everything else" (Acts 17:25). He "causes his sun to rise on the evil and the good, and sends rain on the righteous and the unrighteous" (Matthew 5:45). Yet, those who prefer to manage things on their own may discover that they get their wish. Or, as a result of undeserved mercy, they may find that they are left to manage things themselves until things become so unmanageable that they finally cry out to God for help.

The good news is that when we finally turn to him, we will not find him to be spiteful. Christ will not string us along and leave us wondering whether we will be accepted. He does not say, "You have acted as if you could get along without me for so long that you can wait a little longer." Instead, his response is the same as the father in the parable of the prodigal son. When the son "was still a long way off, his father saw him and was filled with compassion for him; he ran to his son, threw his arms around him and kissed him" (Luke 15:20).

Some of us are troubled by this response. It does not seem fair or responsible. That was certainly the perspective of the prodigal son's older brother, who was so busy toeing the line that he almost thought of himself as a slave. Luke 15:28–30 says that when his father welcomed his lost son back with a feast, the older brother refused to attend. "Look! All these years I've been slaving for you and never disobeyed your orders. Yet you never gave me even a young goat so I could celebrate with my friends," he complained. "But when this son of yours who has squandered your property with prostitutes comes home, you kill the fattened calf for him!"

We can feel similarly when it comes to prayer. Sometimes it seems as if God bestows answers too quickly on those who have ignored him. They are excited about every answer to prayer. It is as if they have discovered a world that they did not know existed, and in a way, they have. We are excited with them, at first. But after a while, there is something about their praise reports that may irk us. We have been praying for many of the same things and are still waiting. Why do their answers seem to come so quickly? Surely, it cannot be that they have more faith than us?

It is possible, of course, that they do have more faith. In Jesus's day, it seemed that those who knew the most about Scripture also had the greatest trouble believing him. Faith does not always correlate with learning or spiritual age. Some who know relatively little in comparison to us may outstrip us in faith. Those who have walked with Christ a long time are sometimes still weak in faith. But this is not the only, or even the primary, reason for the difference. God's dealings with us are personal in the realm of prayer, just as they are in everything else. God is not a vending machine that thoughtlessly dispenses the blessings we want when we place our prayers in the payment slot. Neither is he a kind of heavenly bureaucrat who doles out the same portion to those standing in the prayer line. God's answers are suited to his purposes for us as much as they are to our needs.

According to John 21:22–23, when the risen Christ foretold the kind of death Peter would have, the apostle saw John nearby. "Lord, what about him?" Peter asked. Jesus answered, "If I want him to remain alive until I return, what is that to you? You must follow me." He would say the same, if we asked for an explanation about his answers to our prayers. The fact that God answers one person's prayer a certain way does not mean that he must answer ours the same way. God is obligated only to his own promises. Even then, he may choose to fulfill those promises differently depending upon the individual's need and his own kingdom purposes.

Prayer is an act of faith, and its expectation is shaped by hope. Hope in the common vernacular is more like a wish. We say things like, "I hope it doesn't rain," or "I hope I don't get sick." The hope that springs from faith shares the same spirit of desire but with a much stronger expectation. This hope is closer to certainty. Faith is a kind of motion that leans in God's direction. Hope is the experience that the leaning of faith produces. Between the two, it is faith that is primary because it is the confidence that energizes hope. "Hope, for the Christian, is not wishful thinking or mere blind optimism," New Testament scholar N. T. Wright explains. "It is a mode of knowing, a mode within which new things are possible, options are not shut down, new creation can happen."[7]

Hope is a mode of knowing, but it is a kind of certainty that can hold on to its expectation without demanding to know all the details. There is still much that we do not know. In 1 John 3:2–3 this promise is made: "Dear friends, now we are children of God, and what we will be has not yet been made known. But we know that when Christ appears, we shall be like him, for we shall see him as he is. All who have this hope in him purify themselves, just as he is pure."

We do not yet know the specifics of what our life will be like in eternity. How will we spend our time? What will worship be like? We have been granted a few glimpses in the book of Revelation but not anything like a map or an itinerary. Instead of details, many of which we would probably like to know, John urges us to fix our hope on two basic facts: we are now God's children, and when Christ appears, we shall be like him. This is enough hope to motivate us to action. Those who possess such a hope "purify themselves, just as he is pure."

The Christian's hope does not need to have all the details spelled out to be an "anchor for the soul" (Hebrews 6:19). This is because it is relational. Our hope is anchored to the person and promises of Christ. We are confident not because we have all the information we would like, but because we know that he is trustworthy. We still have questions and uncertainties. We may even have doubts, but we do not doubt him.

What is true of eternity is also true when it comes to prayer. We do not have to know all the details to pray in hope. We do not need to know the specifics of how God may answer us to be confident of his answer. We can be confident that God will answer our prayer and that his answer will be good for us, even if the answer is no. We tend to dwell on the details. We feel that we need to be sure that we will get what we want. We try to visualize the answer and feel positive about the outcome. But the biblical writers urge us to focus our gaze elsewhere. We may not know how God will answer us, but we do know what he has promised. We also know what God has done. These are enough to enable us to say, along with the psalmist, "Why, my soul, are you down-cast? Why so disturbed within me? Put your hope in God, for I will yet praise him, my Savior and my God" (Psalm 42:5, 11; 43:5).

The psalmist's confession of faith is a reminder that our faith must sometimes coexist with questioning. The fact that we are downcast or disturbed does not neces-sarily mean that we have no faith. The psalmist's honesty tempers the blunt warning of James 1:6–7. James cannot mean that real Christians never struggle with doubt. Nor can he mean that we never question whether God will answer our prayers. There is too much evidence that says otherwise. Our own experience betrays us. What James does show us is that doubt's only antidote is faith. If doubt is left unchallenged, it will undermine hope and obstruct our prayers.

How, then, do we pray in faith? First, we should not let our questions, fears, or even our doubts keep us from approaching God in prayer. Like the father who brought his son to Jesus, we should be honest about our struggles. If we do not know how to express our doubts, the father's prayer is enough: "Lord, I believe. Help my unbelief."

Second, we should remind ourselves that a little faith is all that is required to pray. We do not have to wait until we become giants in faith. We do not even need great faith to make large requests. Jesus promised that if you have faith as small as a mustard seed, the smallest of seeds, nothing will be impossible for you (Matthew 17:20).

Third, do not let the size of your request intimidate you. As the old hymn by John Newton says, "Thou art coming to a King, large petitions with thee bring, for His grace and power are such, none can ever ask too much." The answer to your prayer depends upon God, and he is always greater than your request.

Fourth, trust God's timing and plan as you wait for an answer. Even when our requests are the same as those of others, he does not always answer in the same way. His answers are personal, specifically suited to our need and his plan. Jesus urged his disciples to "always pray and not give up" (Luke 18:1). We should persist in prayer until God's answer is clear to us.

According to Hebrews 11:1, faith is: "confidence in what we hope for and assurance about what we do not see." Assurance does not always mean certainty. Theologian Helmut Thielicke has written, "In our prayers, exactly as in our faith, we need not be anything but what we are; on the contrary, we need only be completely what we are."[8]

The key to faith and prayer is to begin with the faith that you have, even if it is only the size of a mustard seed. Anchor your hope to Christ's promise that even the smallest grain of faith is enough to change the shape of the world around you.

Then leave the rest to God.

Questions for Reflection

Chapter 1

KEY TAKEAWAY

Prayer is not like ordinary conversation. It is a conversation that moves primarily in one direction. It moves from the believer who prays to God who hears. God's silence does not mean that he is unresponsive. Listeners are silent when they are paying attention. It is true that in ordinary conversation, silence can also mean other things. When we try to talk to others, they may respond with the silence of disinterest, rejection, or even complete absence. But when it comes to prayer, the first assumption of faith is that we have God's attention.

1. Do you ever find it hard to talk to God? Why or why not?

2. What does prayer have in common with ordinary conversation? How does it differ?

3. In what sense is prayer a one-directional conversation? Is it ever two-directional? Explain your answer.

4. How would you describe your greatest struggle with prayer at this time?

5. What makes special revelation "special"?

6. How might it help us to think of prayer as communion rather than conversation?

7. What can we do to make sure our expectations in prayer are grounded in truth rather than feeling?

8. What advice would you give to someone who doesn't feel like praying? Are there steps you take when you feel this way?

PRAYER

Heavenly Father, before a word is on my tongue you, Lord, know it completely. I long to converse with you. Help me when I find it hard to talk to you. Give me the grace to see your silence as a sign of your presence. Enable me to give voice to my thoughts, concerns, and praise. In Jesus's name, Amen.

Chapter 2

KEY TAKEAWAY

There is more to praying than getting what we want. God has made remarkable promises about the efficacy of prayer, but he retains the right of refusal. He does not always give us what we want, but he will always act on our behalf. The first principle in prayer is to ask. State it as simply as you can. The second is to pray honestly. The third is to persist. Pray and do not give up. God hears us whenever we cry out to him.

1. What was the last prayer that God answered for you? Were you surprised by his answer? Why or why not?

2. Does God ever seem reluctant to answer your prayers? Why does God sometimes seem slow?

3. List some of the reasons God responds to our requests with a refusal. Is it because of us? Why or why not?

4. How would you describe the basic principles that shape the way you pray? Where do they come from? Why are they important to you?

5. The answers to our prayers are an accomplished fact even before they have been granted. Does this make you feel encouraged? Why or why not?

6. How do you think your prayer life will be affected by the knowledge that we are both living in time and in eternity through our relationship with Christ and his redemptive work?

7. Three principles for prayer are named in this chapter (ask, pray honestly, and persist). What are some of the ways you can incorporate these into your prayer life?

PRAYER

Heavenly Father, I am grateful for the many times you have answered my prayers. Remind me of those answers when I grow impatient. Open my eyes to the wisdom of your timing. I wait for you. Your name and renown are the desires of my heart. In Jesus's name, Amen.

Chapter 3

KEY TAKEAWAY

When we pray for others, we are doing more than delivering a grocery list to God. We enter into their struggle and offer genuine help through our prayers—not bargaining or talking God into or out of something. Intercessory prayer is more than a formality. Instead of carefully crafted arguments intended to persuade a reluctant God, we confess God's promises. His grace, mercy, and justice shape our petitions. The more we know about those for whom we pray, the easier it is to be specific. The more we know about God, the more confidently and intelligently we can pray.

1. How often do you pray for people other than yourself? What prompts you to pray for them? How do you pray?

2. It is tempting to view intercessory prayer as an attempt to persuade or bargain with God. What is wrong with this view?

3. Do the stories about Abraham's prayers for God's people encourage you in your prayer life? If so, how?

4. How does prayer enable us to enter into the struggle of others? Why is this an encouragement to pray?

5. When I was a pastor, I was surprised at how frequently people asked me to pray for them, as if my prayers carried more weight with God than their own. Do you feel that the prayers of others carry more weight with God than your own? Why or why not?

6. What are some practical ways to improve your prayers for other people?

7. Who do you feel needs your prayers the most today? Why?

8. What would you like others to pray about for you?

PRAYER

Father of mercies, bring to mind those who need my prayers. Do not let me be discouraged by the magnitude of their need. It is not too big for you. Meet them in distress, calm them in their fears, and provide for them through your power and strength. In Jesus's name, Amen.

Chapter 4

KEY TAKEAWAY

The angry prayers of the Bible are proof that we can share our anger with God. There is more power in prayer than venting on social media. When we express our longing for justice to God in prayer, we invite God to intervene in the situation. It is a form of social action. Yet the teaching of Christ is clear that part of the work of obedience is to take our anger in hand and submit it to the grace of God.

1. How does anger affect your prayers? Do you find it hard to pray for those with whom you are angry? How do you talk to God when you are angry with him?

2. Do you think it is appropriate to ask God to punish those who have harmed you? Why or why not? What is the difference between a prayer for protection from your enemies and a prayer that asks God to judge them?

3. How do you feel about the statement: "Our model is not the imprecatory prayers of the Psalms and Prophets, but the pattern Christ gave us in the Sermon on the Mount"? Does it change how you pray?

4. What do you think John meant when he said that "grace and truth came through Jesus Christ" (John 1:17)? How should truth shape your prayers for those who are your enemies? How should grace shape them?

5. Think of someone with whom you are angry or who has hurt you. What kinds of things would you pray for them right now?

6. You read that "our eagerness to see others held accountable blinds us to the grace that God has shown to us." Can you think of a time when God showed grace to you? How do you feel about God extending grace to your enemy? In what ways does God's extravagant grace impact your prayer life?

7. The obligation to love our enemies does not negate any call for justice for the abused, hungry, poor, sick, or abandoned. How should this affect how we pray for those we consider our enemies?

PRAYER

God of justice, you are my savior and defender. Guard the weak. Rescue the oppressed. Protect the interests of the marginalized. Judge the wicked. I stand in awe of your deeds in the past, Lord. Renew them in our day; in our time make them known, but in wrath remember mercy. In Jesus's name, Amen.

Chapter 5

KEY TAKEAWAY

Everybody who learns to pray begins by praying words they have heard from others. In a way, none of us begins by praying in our own voice. We must first learn a vocabulary and pattern of speech. It shows us what to ask for and how to ask. It enables us to put into words the feelings and desires for which we previously had no name. Over time, what once sounded to us like an unfamiliar voice eventually becomes a way to find our own.

1. What was the first prayer you ever learned by heart? Who taught it to you? Do you still pray it today? Why or why not?

2. Who do you know that prays well? What is it about the way that they pray that impresses you?

3. What role has imitation played in helping you to know how to pray? How has it helped you? What problems, if any, has imitation created for you where prayer is concerned?

4. Is it better to pray using the words of someone else or your own words? Why?

5. Do you usually think of singing as prayer?
   Why or why not? What could your church
   do to make its singing more prayer-like?

6. What do you do when you don't know how
   to pray?

7. What resources, if any, do you turn to that
   provide you with a vocabulary for prayer?

PRAYER

Oh God who hears my prayer, sometimes I fumble for
words when I speak with you. I don't always say what
I mean. Grant that I may give voice to my concerns.
Open my heart to praise you. May the words of my
mouth and the meditation of my heart be pleasing in
your sight, Lord, my Rock and my Redeemer. In Jesus's
name, Amen.

Chapter 6

KEY TAKEAWAY

Prayer requires focus. But perhaps the real problem is that what we call tedium is often familiarity. We have come to prayer looking for a burning bush only to find a quiet room and a comfortable chair. God does not have to announce his arrival with a flourish. He is always with us because he dwells in us (John 14:17). Our momentary conversation does not have to be dramatic. It is enough to say our piece and go our way.

1. When do you find it most difficult to concentrate during prayer? What distracts you?

2. Do you have a strategy for dealing with these distractions? If so, what do you think is helpful?

3. In Ephesians 6:18 Paul mentions "all kinds of prayers." How many kinds of prayer can you identify?

4. How do these different kinds of prayer differ from one another? In what ways do these differences affect the way that you pray?

5. What role does planning have in your prayer life? How might planning your prayers help you to pray better?

6. Do you feel that posture and gestures are important to prayer? Why or why not?

7. What should you do when you find prayer boring? Are there steps you can take to make it less dull?

8. Why doesn't prayer need to be exciting to be effective?

PRAYER

Heavenly Father, help me to focus my attention when I pray. When my mind drifts, draw it back to you. As cares and worries distract me, enable me to cast them upon you. I am thankful for your patient attention to my prayers. In Jesus's name, Amen.

Chapter 7

KEY TAKEAWAY

The Lord's Prayer ends with God just as it begins with him. This is what is at the heart of every prayer. When we pray, we focus our attention on God. We remind ourselves of who he is and what he is like. As we approach him, we place ourselves, our concerns, and even our sins before him. The confidence we have in doing so comes from the fact that it is Jesus Christ who has taught us to pray this way. He is our mentor in prayer. But more than this, he is our passport into God's presence.

1. Christians have viewed the Lord's Prayer as a prayer to be prayed and as a kind of template. Which do you think is its primary function? Why do you think this?

2. When do you recite the Lord's Prayer? Have you thought about why you are saying it?

3. Jesus referred to God as "Father." How does it feel to think of God in such a familiar way?

4. What do you think it means to "hallow" God's name? How is this related to the request for God's kingdom to come?

5. Why do you think Jesus mentions bread before the more spiritual requests for forgiveness and spiritual protection?

6. Jesus speaks of our sins as debts. To whom is the debt owed? How is it paid?

7. Why does Jesus focus so much on forgiving others in connection with his teaching on prayer?

8. When should Christians pray the Lord's Prayer? Why?

PRAYER

Our Father in heaven, may your name be treated as holy. I long for your kingdom to come, so that your will is done on earth as it is in heaven. Give me what I need to live today. Forgive my sins and enable me to forgive those who sin against me. Do not allow me to be overcome by temptation but deliver me from the evil one. In Jesus's name, Amen.

Chapter 8

KEY TAKEAWAY

Silence and prayer may seem antithetical, but God is as comfortable with our silence as he is with his own. Silence is a language that God understands. When we cannot pray for ourselves, Jesus Christ and the Holy Spirit pray for us.

1. In what situations do you most often find yourself at a loss for words? Do you ever find that you have nothing to say to God? Explain.

2. A popular song says that tears are a language that God understands. In what other non-verbal ways do we communicate with God?

3. Which nonverbal ways do you use most often when you are at a loss for words in prayer?

4. Do you find it difficult to sit in silence? Why or why not?

5. Someone has said that we are afraid of silence. Why do you think this is?

6. How does our discomfort with silence affect our prayer lives? Is there anything we can do about this?

7. Do I need to feel that Jesus and the Holy Spirit are praying for me in order for their work to take place? Explain your answer.

8. Is it ever wrong to pray? When might it be better to take action than to pray?

PRAYER

God of creation, the heavens declare the glory of God, but there are times when I am at a loss for words. Could you help me to know what to say? In silence, grant me peace and a sense of your presence. In Jesus's name, Amen.

Chapter 9

KEY TAKEAWAY

According to Hebrews 11:1, faith is "confidence in what we hope for and assurance about what we do not see." Assurance does not always mean certainty. Theologian Helmut Thielicke has written, "In our prayers, exactly as in our faith, we need not be anything but what we are; on the contrary, we need only be completely what we are." The key to faith and prayer is to begin with the faith that you have, even if it is only the size of a mustard seed. Anchor your hope to Christ's promise that even the smallest grain of faith is enough to change the shape of the world around you. Then leave the rest to God.

1. How would you define faith? How would you define doubt?

2. Is doubt the same as uncertainty? How certain do you need to be in prayer?

3. Have you had times of doubt in your walk with Jesus? Explain if, and how, it affected your prayer life.

4. What is the difference between feeling and faith? Are different degrees of faith a matter of feeling?

5. How would explain the fact that not every-
    one has the same degree of faith?

6. How much faith is needed to be effective in
    prayer? Does this mean that our faith doesn't
    matter? Why or why not?

7. What is the relationship between the size of
    our request and the size of our faith?

PRAYER

Heavenly Father, without faith, it is impossible to please
you. Lord, I believe. Help me when I struggle with unbelief. Expand the bounds of my faith so that I might see
the hope to which you have called me and experience
your incomparably great power you have promised to
those who believe. In Jesus's name, Amen.

Notes

INTRODUCTION

1.   C. S. Lewis, *Letters to Malcolm: Chiefly on Prayer* (New York: HarperCollins, 1963), 85.

CHAPTER I: AWKWARD CONVERSATIONS WITH GOD

1.   John Newton, "Come, My Soul, Thy Suit Prepare," in *Hymns to the living God* (Fort Worth: Religious Affections Ministries, 2017), 220.

2.   Helmut Thielicke, *Life Can Begin Again* (Philadelphia: Fortress, 1963), 101.

3.   Thielicke, *Life Can Begin Again*, 105.

4.   Cheslyn Jones, Geoffrey Wainwright, and Edward Yarnold, SJ, *The Study of Spirituality* (New York: Oxford, 1986), 26.

5.   Martyn Lloyd-Jones, *Spiritual Depression: Its Causes and Cure* (Grand Rapids: Eerdmans, 1965), 20.

6.   Robert D. Bergen, *1, 2 Samuel* (Nashville: Broadman & Holman, 1996), 336.

7.   Eugene H. Peterson, *Working the Angles: The Shape of Pastoral Integrity*, (Grand Rapids: Eerdmans, 1987), 33.

8.   "How Firm a Foundation," by John Rippon. Public Domain.

9.   John Stott, *Christian Counter-Culture: The Message of the Sermon on the Mount* (Downers Grove, IL: InterVarsity, 1978), 133–34.

CHAPTER 2: PRAYING AND GETTING WHAT YOU WANT ... OR NOT

1.   B. B. Warfield, "The Importunate Widow," in *Selected Shorter Writings of Benjamin B. Warfield*, vol. II (Phillipsburg, NJ: Presbyterian and Reformed Publishing Company, 1973), 701.

2.   Warfield, "The Importunate Widow," 701.

3.   Warfield, "The Importunate Widow," 703.

4.   C. S. Lewis, "The Efficacy of Prayer," in *The World's Last Night and Other Essays* (San Diego: Harcourt Brace Jovanovich, 1960), 9.

5.   Lewis, "Efficacy of Prayer," 10.

6.   Helmut Thielicke, *Our Heavenly Father* (New York: Harper, 1960), 87.

7.   Thielicke, *Our Heavenly Father*, 84.

8.   Lewis, *Letters to Malcolm*, 27.

CHAPTER 3: THE ART OF PRAYING FOR OTHERS

1. Derek Kidner, *Genesis* (Downers Grove, IL: InterVarsity Press, 1967), 133.

2. Brevard S. Childs, *The Book of Exodus* (Philadelphia: Westminster John Knox, 1974), 556.

3. C. E. B. Cranfield, *The Epistle to the Romans, Vol. II* (Edinburgh: T&T Clark, 1979), 777.

4. Gordon P. Wiles, *Paul's Intercessory Prayers: The Significance of the Intercessory Prayer Passages in the Letters of St. Paul* (London: Cambridge University Press, 1974), 155.

5. J. C. Ryle, *Home Truths: Being Miscellaneous Tracts and Addresses* (London: William Hunt, 1887), 130.

6. Lewis, "The Efficacy of Prayer," 9.

7. Wiles, *Paul's Intercessory Prayers*, 29.

8. Eusebius, *The Ecclesiastical History*, book II, chapter XXIII, translated by Kirsopp Lake (Cambridge: Harvard, 1975), 171.

CHAPTER 4: MANAGING OUR ANGRY PRAYERS

1. Michael Widmer, *Standing in the Breach: An Old Testament Theology and Spirituality of Intercessory Prayer* (Winona Lake, IN: Eisenbrauns, 2015), 3.

2. John R. W. Stott, *Christian Counter-Culture: The Message of the Sermon on the Mount* (Downers Grove, IL: InterVarsity Press, 1978), 105.

3. Walter Brueggemann, *Praying the Psalms* (Winona, MN: Saint Mary's Press, 1982), 79.

4. Brueggemann, *Praying the Psalms*, 79.

5. Eugene Peterson, *Under the Unpredictable Plant* (Grand Rapids: Eerdmans, 1992), 157.

6. Peterson, *Under the Unpredictable Plant*, 194.

CHAPTER 5: PRAYING IN THE
WORDS OF ANOTHER

1. Lewis, *Letters to Malcolm*, 86.

2. Andrew B. McGowan, *Ancient Christian Worship: Early Church Practices in Social, Historical, and Theological Perspective* (Grand Rapids: Baker, 2014), 191.

3. Augustine, *The Teacher*, in *Augustine: Earlier Writings*, ed. J. H. S. Burleigh (Philadelphia: Westminster John Knox, 1953), 70.

4. Augustine, *The Teacher*, 184.

5. Joachim Jeremias, *The Prayers of Jesus* (Philadelphia: Fortress, 1984), 79.

6. Jeremias, *The Prayers of Jesus*, 79.

7. Jeremias, *The Prayers of Jesus*, 70.

8. Michael W. Holmes, *The Apostolic Fathers: Greek Text and English Translations*, 3rd ed. (Grand Rapids: Baker, 2007), 357.

9.   Holmes, *The Apostolic Fathers*, 359.

10. Holmes, *The Apostolic Fathers*, 359, 361.

11. Holmes, *The Apostolic Fathers*, 361.

12. Eugene Peterson, *Eat This Book: A Conversation in the Art of Spiritual Reading* (Grand Rapids: Eerdmans, 2006), 105–6.

13. Joachim Jeremias, *The Eucharistic Words of Jesus* (Philadelphia: Fortress, 1966), 256.

14. Peterson, *Eat This Book*, 105.

15. Peter Davids, *The Epistle of James* (Chicago: Moody, 1982), 191.

16. Douglas Moo, *The Letter of James* (Downers Grove, IL: InterVarsity Press, 1985), 175.

17. Michael O'Connor, "The Singing of Jesus," in *Resonant Witness: Conversations Between Music and Theology*, ed. Jeremy Begbie and Steven R. Guthrie (Grand Rapids: Eerdmans, 2011), 440.

18. O'Connor, "The Singing of Jesus," 442–43.

19. McGowan, *Ancient Christian Worship*, 111.

20. Jeremy S. Begbie, *Resounding Truth: Christian Wisdom in the World of Music* (Grand Rapids: Baker, 2007), 47.

21. John Calvin, *Institutes of the Christian Religion*, ed. John T. McNeill, trans. Ford Lewis Battles (Philadelphia: Westminster, 1960), 895.

22.   Thomas Troeger, *Wonder Reborn: Creating Sermons on Hymns, Music, and Poetry* (New York: Oxford, 2010), 29.

23.   Troeger, *Wonder Reborn*, 29.

24.   James K. A. Smith, *Desiring the Kingdom: Worship, Worldview, and Cultural Formation* (Grand Rapids: Baker, 2009), 86–86.

25.   Smith, *Desiring the Kingdom*, 152.

CHAPTER 6: HOW TO STAY FOCUSED DURING PRAYER

1.   John Calvin, *Institutes of the Christian Religion, Vol. II*, edited by John T. McNeill, Trans. Ford Lewis Battles, III, XX, 5 (Philadelphia: Westminster, 1960), 854.

2.   Donald K. Smith, *Creating Understanding: A Handbook for Christian Communication Across Cultural Landscapes* (Grand Rapids: Zondervan, 1992), 154.

3.   McGowan, *Ancient Christian Worship*, 193.

4.   Geoffrey Wainwright, *Eucharist and Eschatology* (New York: Oxford, 1981), 78–79.

5.   Robert Wuthnow, *All in Sync: How Music and Art Are Revitalizing American Religion* (Berkeley: University of California), 131–32.

6.   Wuthnow, *All in Sync*, 84.

7.   Anthony Bloom, *Beginning to Pray* (Mahwah, NJ: Paulist Press, 1970), 45.

CHAPTER 7: JESUS ON PRAYER

1. The closing phrase which ascribes kingdom, power, and glory to the Father appears as a footnote in the NIV because it does not appear in the earliest manuscripts of Matthew's Gospel, but it has traditionally been prayed by the church.

2. Helmut Thielicke, *The Prayer that Spans the World*, trans. John W. Doberstein (Cambridge: James Clarke & Co., 1953), 55.

3. McGowan, *Ancient Christian Worship*, 186.

4. Didache 8:3

5. McGowan, *Ancient Christian Worship*, 171.

6. Jeremias, *The Prayers of Jesus*, 12–13.

7. John Calvin, *A Harmony of the Gospels Matthew, Mark, and Luke Vol. I*, trans. A. W. Morrison (Grand Rapids: Eerdmans, 1972), 203–4.

8. McGowan, *Ancient Christian Worship*, 190–91.

9. Jeremias, *The Prayers of Jesus*, 98.

10. John Nolland, *The Gospel of Matthew: A Commentary on the Greek Text* (Grand Rapids: Eerdmans, 2005), 287.

11. Thielicke, *The Prayer that Spans the World*, 75.

12. Thielicke, *The Prayer that Spans the World*, 75.

13. Jeremias, *The Prayers of Jesus*, 103.

14. Didache 8:2.

CHAPTER 8: PRAYERS WITHOUT WORDS

1.   Stephen H. Webb, *The Divine Voice: Christian Proclamation and the Theology of Sound* (Grand Rapids: Brazos, 2004), 222.

2.   Jacques Ellul, *Reason for Being: A Meditation on Ecclesiastes* (Grand Rapids: Eerdmans, 1990), 272.

3.   William Barclay, *The Letter to the Romans* (Philadelphia: Westminster, 1975), 112.

4.   Herman Ridderbos, *Paul: An Outline of His Theology*, trans. John Richard De Witt (Grand Rapids: Eerdmans, 1975), 227–28.

5.   "My Shepherd Will Supply My Need," by Isaac Watts. Public Domain.

CHAPTER 9: FAITH, HOPE, AND PRAYER

1.   C. E. B. Cranfield, *The Epistle to the Romans, Vol. I* (Edinburgh: T&T Clark, 1975), 100.

2.   C. K. Barrett, *A Commentary on the Epistle to the Romans* (New York: Harper & Row, 1957), 31.

3.   Joachim Jeremias, *New Testament Theology* (New York: Scribner's Sons, 1971), 163.

4.   Jeremias, *New Testament Theology*, 164.

5.   Jeremias, *New Testament Theology*, 163.

6. John Ker, "Faith's Approach to Christ," in *Classic Sermons on Faith and Doubt*, ed. Warren W. Wiersbe (Grand Rapids: Hendrickson, 1991), 93.

7. N. T. Wright, *Surprised by Hope: Rethinking Heaven, the Resurrection, and the Mission of the Church* (New York: HarperOne, 2008), 72.

8. Helmut Thielicke, *Christ and the Meaning of Life: Sermons and Meditations* (London: James Clarke & Co., 1962), 102.